# The End of All Things

# THE
# END
# OF ALL
# THINGS

A Defense of the Future

C. JONATHIN SERAIAH

Canon Press

MOSCOW, IDAHO

Thanks first of all to my wife, Cathy, for just being there and for the encouragement, support and understanding, you are truly "bone of my bones, and flesh of my flesh," and I thank God for you daily; to Mark Cave, an Elder who "holds fast to the Word"; thanks for asking me, "Why don't you write a book about it?" Sorry that you had to spend so much time fixing the "computer from the abyss"; to the members of Bible Fellowship Church, I love you all; thanks for letting me break all the "rules"; to Doug Jones, for being interested in the first place (what does your name spell in Sanskrit?) and for all the wonderful editorial help—let's do it again sometime; and last, but not least, to the King of kings and Lord of lords, for Your incomprehensible grace and mercy to a sinner like me.

C. Jonathin Seraiah
*The End of All Things: A Defense of the Future*

© 1999 by C. Jonathin Seraiah
Published by Canon Press, P.O. Box 8741, Moscow, ID 83843
800–488–2034 / www.canonpress.org

03 02 01 00 99   9 8 7 6 5 4 3 2 1

Printed in the United States of America

Cover design by Paige Atwood Design, Moscow, ID

Cover painting: central panel cross section of *The Last Judgment*, Hieronymus Bosch, c. 1435–1516. Oil on panel. Akademie der Bildenden Künste, Vienna. Photo copyright © 1999 The Art Resource, New York, NY.

Unless otherwise indicated, Scripture quotations are from the *Revised Standard Version* of the Bible; copyright © by the National Council of Churches of Christ in America. Scripture quotations marked NIV are from the New International Version of the Bible; copyright © by the International Bible Society 1984. Those marked NAS are from the New American Standard; copyright © by the Lockman Foundation 1977.

ISBN: 1-885767-53-6

To Lou,
my "perfect one,"
let me slay another dragon.

# Contents

# Foreword

**by R.C. Sproul Jr.**

What would you do if you had the cure for a sickness that debilitated thousands? Now suppose that this cure of yours, if taken in too strong a dose, were fatal? There is an antidote, but those given to taking the fatal dose deny that such exists. If you could, I presume you would go back to your lab and see if you couldn't find something equally effective in combatting the sickness, but that is not quite so dangerous for those who refuse to read the warnings on your bottle.

C. Jonathin Seraiah has done just that. The sickness that is epidemic in the evangelical church is the disease of dispensationalism, and more particularly dispensational eschatology. These doctrines not only twist and distort the Scripture but bring the church to near paralysis. The harder we work to build Christ's kingdom, the more we delay it.

Thankfully, God in his mercy has done a great work in waking up many people to their condition. The rapid spread of the doctrine of preterism has been a welcome tonic. No more visits to the chiropractor after making "some of you will not sleep" and "this generation shall not pass" stretch out into two millennia. The sad news is that as more people begin to take seriously Christ's promise to return within a generation of His speaking, more people have swallowed the fatal dose of pantelism, the doctrine that all biblical prophecy has been fulfilled. This doctrine is fatal because it denies not only the return of Christ but also the resurrection of our bodies.

Too many people have leaned away from the briar patch of dispensationalism on their left only to fall from their horse into the pit of the damnable heresy of pantelism on their right.

Many of us, in doing battle with the pantelists, have been using powerful weapons that aren't quite powerful enough. We warn the pantelists that they have strayed from the confessions of the Church since its beginning. They just yawn and remind us that we ourselves confess that confessions can err.

Mr. Seraiah has taken a better approach. He has brought to bear the sword of the Lord, making his case against pantelism exegetically rather than creedally. Verse by verse, precept upon precept, he argues that Scripture not only may but must proclaim a future coming of Christ and the final resurrection of our bodies. He answers the Scripture twisting of the pantelists with straight Scripture. He deftly wields that sword and stays aright upon the horse.

But his work is not finished. Having dispatched error with Scripture alone, Mr. Seraiah wisely goes back to sharpen the creeds, to explain that while they can err, they nevertheless define historic orthodoxy. Having won the battle with one hand tied behind his back, he reminds us there still is that other hand.

It is my earnest prayer that many in the pantelist camp are merely temporarily theologically lost and not forever outside the faith. I pray they just got a little carried away, that they still might hear the voice of the still-coming Shepherd. If so, here are the call and the directions to come home. Christ has died. Christ has risen. Christ will come again.

# Introduction

THE SOULLESS LIBERALISM OF THE NINETEENTH CENTURY LEFT many people with a firm desire to return to a solid understanding of the Scriptures. But rather than returning to the sound teaching of the previous centuries, many believers sought out new teachings, especially in eschatology. We were told that all the "signs" of the Second Coming were coming to pass and thus that Jesus was definitely going to return within a few years. This teaching spread like wildfire (due mostly to the onset of the Scofield Reference Bible), and eventually these views took on the name "dispensationalism." One of dispensationalism's foremost characteristics was and is to read *all* prophecies in the New (and usually the Old) Testament as referring to the Final Advent of Christ.

Over the past few decades, dispensationalism itself has faced increasing critical re-evaluation. As many believers have been moved to delve deeper into the scriptural basis for dispensational teachings, they have often come to the conclusion that dispensationalism has missed the mark drastically. In addition, many of those who have done this have been discovering that both the liberals and dispensationalists were misdirected along the same path. Liberalism said, "Jesus was wrong to say His return was soon." Dispensationalism said, "Jesus never said His return was to be soon in the first century but soon in the twentieth century."

Today, a growing group of evangelicals wants to take the exegetical good of both the liberals and the dispensationalists. They argue that Jesus did say His final return was in the first century (as per liberalism), and that He was right in what He said (as per dispensationalism). In their response, however, they have gone to the opposite extreme. The dispensationalists moved all the references to Jesus' "coming" to today. This new group wants to move *all* the references to Jesus' "coming" to the first century and say that it really did happen then. Their error is the same as that of the dispensationalists and the liberals (both of whom they want to oppose). They don't carefully let the distinctions in the references to Jesus' return speak for themselves. Both groups tend to make this debate a simplistic matter of brute, logical consistency—all then or all now. But Scripture is not that simplistic.

## A Radical Distinction

Though the dispensationalists were clearly wrong in much of their eschatology, they have maintained a belief in the Final Advent of Christ, a future, physical Resurrection, and the Day of Judgment. Our "new" group has denied the historic understanding of these doctrines. In this case they have rejected the errors of dispensationalism for errors that are far worse.

Throughout history, the primary creeds that have been used by the Spirit to unite the Church (the Apostles' and the Nicene) have affirmed the three essential doctrines of the Final Advent, the physical Resurrection, and the Day of Judgment. This is certainly not to be taken lightly.

This "new" teaching I speak of strongly desires to separate itself from the sort of exegetical fallacies in the writings of Hal Lindsey and the like. Even those within dispensationalism are seeing the need to rethink much of what has been taught for years now. I can attest to this situation in my own life. I started off as a dispensationalist (it was the only thing I had heard at first). As years went by, I began to recognize that the Scriptures did not support what I believed; I began a long and slow journey to find what the Scriptures really did say about the Second Coming. After years of prayer and study, I too have found myself disagreeing with dispensationalism on numerous grounds.

### "Pantelism"

The new teaching which has arisen in response to dispensationalism has been referred to by its adherents as "fulfilled eschatology" and sometimes as "consistent preterism" (*preter* means *past*). Of course, no one wants to be "inconsistent," so they have made their opponents' position in error by definition. Christian communication can occur much more easily if we accept terms that appropriately define where we stand. In addition, the position presented in this book is that they are only consistent (in most cases) within their own system (which is not difficult—you merely relegate everything in Scripture to the past before you examine it). They are not consistent with Scripture itself. "Preterist" is obviously insufficient as a term for this group because they themselves find the need to add qualifiers like "consistent" to it.

Therefore, desiring to make an easy reference to this group that they themselves might accept, I shall refer to this movement as "pantelism" (from the Greek words meaning "all is completed"), and I will use the term "preterism" exclusively for those who hold that most of the eschatology of the New Testament is past. Since the term "preterist" refers to the "past," and "pantelist" means clearly "all is past," and the term "preterist" has not been used historically to refer to "pantelists," I believe this is a fair distinction. I have done this with a desire to distinguish these two groups and to make their individual stances more clear in their names. We must remember here that in a certain sense every Christian is preterist; what makes us Christians is that we believe the prophecy about the (first) coming of the Messiah is past. Every Christian has at least some preterist beliefs. Thus "preterist" is an insufficient term to describe those who hold that all of the prophecies of the Bible were fulfilled by A.D. 70.

It is true that the "eschatology" of the New Testament is predominantly preterist. For those unfamiliar with the preterist perspective, it is the ancient view that many of the eschatological passages of the New Testament were fulfilled (completely) in the destruction of Jerusalem in A.D. 70. This view may sound novel, but in reality there have been orthodox adherents to it throughout church history (e.g., Clement of Alexandria, Eusebius, John Lightfoot, John Owen, Milton Terry, Jay Adams). This interpretation does not deny the Final Coming of Christ; it merely finds that not all "coming" passages refer to that event. The preterist interpretation is actually the most faithful to the biblical text because it recognizes that Old Testament prophetic terminology was used by the New Testament authors. This recognition is helpful in distinguishing the prophecies of Christ's coming that were near, in the first century (Matt. 10:23; 16:28; 24:30; 26:64; 1 Thess. 5:2; 2 Thess. 1:7; James 5:7–9; 1 Pet. 4:7; Rev. 1:3, 7; etc.) and thus fulfilled in A.D. 70, from those that were far (John 5:28–29; Acts 1:11; 17:31; 1 Cor. 15:23–24; 1 Thess. 4:16; 1 Jn. 3:2; etc.) and thus not yet fulfilled even in our day. It also helps to distinguish between a spiritual "coming" (invisible for temporal judgment, as in A.D. 70) and a physical coming (visible for eternal judgment).

It is not true, however, that the eschatology of the New Testament is exclusively preterist; some prophecies are yet to be fulfilled. But the pantelists have gone so far as to deny the Final Advent of Christ at the end of the world, an end accompanied by the final (physical) Resurrection and Judgment Day. In addition, most have gone on to deny there is a future eternal state. In other words, this is eternity now; we go on like this forever. It is not my desire to ignore the works of those who have gone before me who have put forward an orthodox understanding of the Final Advent of Christ. It is my desire, however, to state that those who are heterodox need to be shown as such and should not be allowed to proclaim heresy as truth within the church of Jesus Christ.

## Theological Ramifications

Many within the church today find the act of departing from various doctrines of the historic Christian faith to be of no terrific consequence. I am not saying one needs have all of his eschatological "ducks in a row" in order to be saved. There are many Christians I admire very much whom I believe to be wrong in their understanding of eschatology.

The issue involved here is that all doctrines (no matter how obscure) affect our relationship with God in some way. If a Christian believes the Bible says the world will be completely destroyed tomorrow, he will act in certain ways he would not act if he believed the world was not going to end until long after his death.

Our salvation is not, of course, based on our understanding of the events related to the first or second coming of Christ. Our salvation is based on what Christ did at His first coming and through our faith in Him. Pantelism, however, is a teaching—growing in evangelical circles today—that can be called nothing other than heresy, and the ramifications of this teaching are not only dangerous for individuals but destructive to the Church of Jesus Christ.

**Chapter One**

# Historical Implausibilities

WHEN WE FIRST CONSIDER PANTELIST ASSUMPTIONS, WE FIND a basic point that is difficult for any Christian to accept: Their contention (whether expressed verbally or not) that the Church has been wrong for two thousand years about such a major doctrine as the Final Advent and only recently has anyone figured out what the Bible was really saying. The presumption about one's abilities that it takes to affirm something of this sort is incredibly high. They are essentially saying the Holy Spirit was unable to properly teach the Church what was really involved in the Second Coming (or was unwilling, and for some bizarre reason decided to leave the Church in the dark and allow her to promote errant theology for two thousand years). The primary danger of this belief is in what else it may allow. Will we find out tomorrow that the Church has been wrong about the deity of Christ?

I certainly do not want to say that the "majority rules" when it comes to Christian truth. I also, however, do not want to say the Holy Spirit died (at least with respect to eschatology) with the last apostle and was resurrected when the first pantelist came on the scene. The history of the Church (although not a history of perfectly inspired actions and beliefs) is still the history of the Holy Spirit. He continues to work in the children of God, drawing them closer and closer to Christ-likeness in both thought and deed (Rom. 8:14; 1 Cor. 2:10–14; Eph. 1:17).

## The Maturity of the Church

According to pantelism, all things must have been fulfilled by A.D. 70. This would include passages like Ephesians 4:11–13 (denoting the perfection of our knowledge of Christ) and 1 Corinthians 13:9–10 (denoting the same thing in different terms) in their entirety. This would lead us to affirm (by pantelist assumptions) that our knowledge was made perfect in an absolute sense, meaning it cannot have anything lacking or in error. The pantelist must be unwilling to allow that anything about the perfection of the church still awaits us today. If there is anything left unfulfilled by A.D. 70 then the pantelist has dug himself a hole too big to get out of (without giving up his pantelism). Thus, given their framework, the Church was brought to a perfect knowledge of Christ in all forms: Scripture, tradition, individual understanding, etc. This is hard enough to swallow by itself. But in addition, if this is so, how did the Church so quickly (once again, according to pantelism) lose that "perfect knowledge" and fall into error by affirming a Final Coming of Christ after A.D. 70? Either her knowledge was perfect and she didn't fall into error, or her knowledge wasn't perfect (and thus there are things left unfulfilled in the first century). Pantelism can't have it both ways.

Another problem with the "two thousand years of error" notion is that the generation of Christians who had seen and heard the teaching of the apostles themselves must have suddenly changed their position on the Second Coming from what the apostles had taught them. They therefore delved into wholesale apostasy in regard to one of the most important teachings of the apostles, rather quickly after A.D. 70, perhaps while some of the apostles were still alive (the apostle John is universally reported by Church tradition to have survived till at least the end of the first century). On pantelist grounds, they were still waiting for Christ to come when He had already done so and was not going to do so again. If there were any who would have known well the teachings of the apostles, it would have been the pastors and elders of the churches, the very ones who had opportunity to preach and write against it. To say the Church forgot what she was taught and underwent a radical change in belief of these proportions is an amazing assertion that cannot stand without some historical evidence.

The Church has certainly seen times of deep error, but she has never gone for long without a testimony of the truth. The pantelists want to say the Church went without a true testimony for even the basics of eschatology for two thousand years. This is indeed an amazing presumption.

## The Church Fathers
At this point it is important to point directly to what the early Church believed in regard to eschatology. There is no doubt that many in the early Church held to a preterist perspective of various Scriptures,[1] and the work of those who have shown this to be so will not be repeated here; this is not my point of contention. We seek rather to see whether the Church held *also* to a coming of Christ that was future to them. Let's therefore examine the evidence for the early Church's belief in a yet-to-occur physical coming of Christ (i.e., post–A.D. 70), as well as its attendant physical Resurrection and Judgment Day.

### First Clement
The writing of 1 Clement is usually dated around A.D. 95 or 96.[2] Though a case can be made to date it as early as the late 60s, the note of the Neronian persecu-

tion being in the past (chap. 5–6) seems to place the
book after this event. Either way it is clear it was written closely within the time of the apostles. The note
that some of those appointed by the apostles are still
living (44:3–5) gives credence to a date most probably
within the first century. The possibility of an early date
will not be ignored. This is one of the reasons why we
have chosen to cover Clement first; if he was writing
before A.D. 70 then some (though not all) of what is
referred to below may actually be speaking about the
destruction of Jerusalem. This point is therefore acknowledged at the beginning. Most of what is said below will assume a post-70 date for the book.

We find in examining 1 Clement that the author
(whose name we shall assume to have been Clement,
though the book itself does not give this name) gives us
a testimony that is quite helpful for our discussion.
Clement was most assuredly alive at the time of the
destruction of Jerusalem (even if he did write in the
90s), and thus he had at least some background knowledge of the events surrounding it (not to mention the
numerous prophecies about it that even nonpreterists
cannot deny—Matt. 21:41; 22:7; 23:37–38; 24:2; Luke
19:42–44; 21:20; Acts 6:14). It is therefore intriguing
to find that he is still looking forward to the return of
Christ and its concurrent developments.

First, we find his interpretation of Psalm 110:1,
1 Corinthians 15:25, and other like passages, which say
that the Father told Jesus, "Sit at my right hand, *till* I
make your enemies your footstool" (emphasis mine).
In 36:5, Clement refers to this as justification for not
being one of Christ's enemies. Hence he believes Christ
is still upon His throne waiting for all of His enemies
to be made His footstool (most particularly the last enemy,
"death," which according to pantelism has already happened[3]). If Christ is viewed by Clement as still on His
throne, then according to the full context in 1 Corin-

thians 15:23–26, he believed the "end" and the "coming" of Christ that Paul is referring to had not yet come in his day.

Clement also makes specific mention of a future Day of Judgment. In 28:1–2, Clement refers to being "sheltered by his mercy from the judgment to come." This shelter is desired because God is omniscient and nothing that we do is unknown to Him (28:3–4). Though he is definitely referring to his quotation of Psalm 19:1–3 in the previous chapter (27:7), one can also easily see an allusion to Romans 2:16, the "day when . . . God judges the secrets of men by Christ Jesus." Once again he is viewing the judgment as including all the deeds of all men everywhere, not just the deeds of those Jews in Jerusalem.

We also can clearly find Clement's belief that there was to be a future physical Resurrection. In 24:1, Clement makes clear reference to "a future resurrection, of which he has made the first-fruits, by raising the Lord Jesus Christ from the dead." He is obviously alluding to 1 Corinthians 15:23 here, which is another indication of the future coming of Christ in Clement's mind. This is because we are told plainly by Paul that it is at Christ's "coming" that He will resurrect believers: "Christ the first fruits, then at his coming those who belong to Christ." Paul's (and Clement's) association between Christ's resurrection and that of the believer's (which will be examined below in detail) shows they are of the same nature—physical. Also in 26:1, Clement notes that it is obvious God "will bring about the resurrection of those who served him in holiness"; again the resurrection is seen as both physical and in the future.

Similarly, we can find an allusion to 1 John 3:3 where the apostle is speaking of a "hope" in the future resurrection that "purifies" the individual. In 27:1, Clement says "in this hope then let our souls be bound to him."

He had just quoted Job 19:26 in the previous chapter
(26:3), which speaks of God raising up this "flesh which
has endured all these things," and so Clement maintains the flow of thought by saying the soul hopes to be
reunited with the flesh in the future. Clement, following John, taught us to hope in a physical resurrection
("we shall be like him"—1 Jn. 3:2), and this hope (in a
right understanding of the Resurrection) has a purifying affect on the believer.

### Second Clement
This letter (probably not written by the same author as
1 Clement) is difficult to date. The most probable date
is somewhere between A.D. 100 and 150, and even this
date has opposition from various sources.[4] It is obvious that this book does not have the situation we find
with 1 Clement; the date of this letter is most definitely after the destruction of Jerusalem. Therefore any
belief the author has of a future return of Christ, Resurrection, and Judgment will be highly significant for
this study.

In 17:4, the author quotes Isaiah 66:18: "I am coming to gather all nations and tongues." The author's words
are as follows: "For the Lord said: 'I come to gather all
the nations, tribes, and languages.' By this he means
the day of his appearing, when he will come and
ransom each of us according to our works." He here
gathers together the future coming of Christ and the
judging of all men.

What is most significant here is that the passage in
Isaiah refers to "all nations" being gathered before the
Lord. This is entirely different from the passages that
refer solely to the destruction of Jerusalem in the first
century. The issue in A.D. 70 was the judgment of the
(single) nation of Israel, not the judgment of all nations
(i.e., all people). "All nations" (or Gentiles) have not
yet been gathered before Christ to be judged by Him.

A few other references help focus on future judgment even more clearly. While discussing the need for good deeds in his hearers, our author reminds them that there is a coming Day of Judgment. It is on this particular day that the author says there "shall be made manifest the secret and open deeds of men" (16:3).

A final important passage on this subject is just a few verses after the previous one. Still discussing the need for repentance from evil deeds, the author says that the statement "their worm shall not die and their fire shall not be quenched" (Is. 66:24) is a reference to what will occur (in the future) on the "day of judgment" (17:5–6).

This also is not merely a temporal judgment as the destruction of Jerusalem was in the first century. The author speaks of the wicked being "punished with terrible torture in unquenchable fire" (17:7); he says this is seen by the righteous who are being blessed. The pains of a temporal torture can easily be quenched when the person dies. The pains, however, of an eternal punishment are never quenched. Once again our author is alluding to a judgment that ushers in an experience of eternity, not merely something that pertains to this life.

In referring to his own position in this need for personal piety, the author gives one primary reason for his effort to pursue "righteousness." It is because of his "fear of the judgment to come" (18:2); he knows that even though judgment was poured out on Israel one last time, there is still a judgment to be brought on all mankind in the future.[5]

The future resurrection was another hope of the author of 2 Clement. Near the end of his letter (or possibly sermon), he seeks to encourage those who are enduring affliction in his day. He tells them they have the hope of the "immortal fruit of the resurrection" (19:3). His description of this involves "a time of blessedness," and he says those resurrected will "live again" in "eternity where there is no sorrow" (19:4). This is unmistakably the same as the orthodox doctrine of the future resurrection.

In an earlier chapter of the book, the author warns his hearers against denying either the future resurrection or the judgment (9:1). He then goes on to prove that this is true, based at least partly on the fact that Christ Himself had physical flesh (9:5). Thus he viewed our resurrection as relating to our physical nature and not merely as something spiritual.

### Ignatius of Antioch

Let us turn now to Ignatius. Though an exact date is impossible, there is today unanimity that Ignatius was writing sometime between 107 and 117.[6] Thus we once again have a situation different from what we have with 1 Clement; if Ignatius looked forward to a coming of Christ, there is no doubt it was post–A.D. 70. In examining Ignatius's thought, however, we have more than one letter to use for information. There are seven letters he wrote to churches and individuals. Despite this, I shall not be examining them independently, since they were written at the same time.

After rejecting the view of those who said that Christ only appeared to suffer (Docetism), Ignatius says, "I know and believe that he was in the flesh even after the Resurrection" (I Sm 3:1) and gives an argument for this belief from the testimony of the Gospels. In a later note, Ignatius says that Christ's resurrection was "of flesh" (I Sm 12:2) to again point out that it was not merely a spiritual event. This shows us that Ignatius definitely views Christ's resurrection as physical, and this helps us to understand how he views the resurrection of all believers. In a separate letter, Ignatius mentions that Christ was "truly"[7] raised from the dead. This leads him to point out that "in the same manner,"[8] believers will someday be raised from the dead (I Tr 9:2). In other words, Ignatius states he is waiting for a resurrection of all believers that is of the same nature Christ's was: physical, eternal, and in defeat of physical death.

### Polycarp

Our next Church father is Polycarp, whom tradition attests to have been a disciple of the apostle John himself. We have only one of Polycarp's letters to use as a source of his thought, but as we will see, that one letter provides a wealth of information for the topic at hand. Polycarp's letter to the Church at Philippi is commonly dated around A.D. 110 for various reasons within the text itself.[9] Most specifically we can date it after the death of Paul because of the clear reference to his death (9:1–2).

Remembering the situation we saw with Clement of Rome and his understanding of 1 Corinthians 15:25, we find a similar situation in Polycarp. In 2:1, Polycarp notes that Christ is (in Polycarp's day) still on His throne at the "right hand" of God Almighty. He has thus not yet "come" and brought the "end," as per the reference Paul makes in Corinthians.

Within the same verse, Polycarp also says that Christ is the "'Judge of the living and of the dead,' whose blood God *will require* from them who disobey him" (emphasis mine). The word Polycarp uses for "require" is a simple future tense;[10] he expected this still to happen.

Within the same context (2:2), Polycarp makes mention of his belief that believers will be resurrected as Christ was: "Now 'he who raised him' from the dead 'will also raise us up.'" This is again a future event he is looking forward to.[11] Thus within one passage we find Polycarp declaring his convictions that (1) Christ was yet to come again, (2) there was yet to be a Judgment Day for all mankind, and (3) there was yet to be a physical resurrection.

Later, Polycarp again makes reference to his belief in a future resurrection. He says that to those who prove themselves faithful and true believers God has promised resurrection. Including himself in that group (and thus denoting it as future to himself), he says God will "raise us from the dead" (5:2).

In another place Polycarp points again to the future judgment.[12] He now calls his readers to live a life of holiness and to forgive others. Polycarp's argument is based on our asking God to forgive us, since He sees all that we do, when we stand before "the judgment seat of Christ" (6:2).

Polycarp, however, goes even one step further in his beliefs. He continues with the context we have just mentioned and states that anyone who denies there is a resurrection and judgment (unequivocally future, as is seen above) is "the first-born of Satan" (7:1). To say Polycarp viewed the Resurrection, Judgment Day, and as a result, the Final Advent as crucial doctrines that a person cannot deny without peril to his salvation is not going too far.

### Epistle of Barnabas

We move next to the Epistle of Barnabas. Whether it was really written by the Barnabas of Acts 4:36 is unknown (and also highly doubtful). Its date is commonly given as "after the destruction of the temple in Jerusalem in A.D. 70."[13] Beyond that it is difficult to put a specific date on the letter. The allegorical approach it takes in a number of passages raises questions for some. This must be admitted at the start. We are therefore looking for teaching that is outside of this allegorical arena. This will be difficult as this is the primary support for much of the author's doctrine.

What we should remember is that one's method of proving what one believes is not the same as the beliefs themselves. Many theologians of the early Church used questionable methods to prove the deity of Christ. It is certainly acceptable to say the author was taught things by people who used theological disciplines other than allegory and that he later came into the allegorical method by which he proves his beliefs. Either way, we shall see that the author of the Epistle of Barnabas agrees with the other church fathers in the area of the Final Advent, Resurrection, and Judgment Day.

The coming of Christ is not a common reference in the epistle, yet we often do find its concomitant events mentioned. There is, however, one reference that clearly mentions the Final Advent of Christ. In 15:5 he writes "when his Son comes he will destroy the time of the wicked one, and will judge the godless . . . and then he will truly rest." Once again this event is looked forward to by the author as future. In this context he is connecting the "coming" of Christ with Judgment Day. It also has a reference that can easily be seen to refer to an end of this present world and the beginning of eternity: "when we enjoy true rest . . . because we have been made righteous ourselves and have received the promise, when there is no more sin, but all things have been made new by the Lord" (15:7).

There are also a number of references to judgment in the epistle that are important for our discussion. We shall merely quote them below:

The Lord will "judge" the world "without respect to persons." (4:12)

The Son of God . . . is "destined to judge the living and the dead." (7:2)

The wicked shall not rise up in judgment. (11:7; cf. Ps 1:5)

Thou shalt remember the day of judgment day and night, and thou shall seek each day the society of saints. (19:10)

> And be taught of God, seeking out what the Lord requires
> from you, and see that ye be found faithful in the day of
> Judgment. (21:6)

The author is evidently concerned about a future day
when both he and his readers were to be judged by Christ
Almighty for their deeds. This is more significant when
we realize the letter firmly emphasizes that the international Church is the true heir to the promises of God.
Writing after the destruction of Jerusalem, he knows
the Jews have already received a full temporal judgment
upon their entire nation. He is waiting for a future judgment that is on a larger scale than that experienced by
Israel.

There are also two clear references that connect the
resurrection with the Judgment as concurrent events
in the future. He views them as two parts of one event;
the glorious resurrection is for the faithful, and the fearful
judgment is for the wicked. This is perfectly in accord
with the Scriptures. Resurrection is used almost exclusively for true believers, whereas judgment is used almost exclusively for the lost.

> He himself will raise the dead and judge the risen. (5:7)

> It is good therefore that he who has learned the ordinances
> of the Lord as many as have been written should walk in
> them. For he who does these things shall be glorified in the
> kingdom of God, and he who chooses the others shall perish
> with his works. For this reason there is a resurrection, for
> this reason there is a recompense. (21:1)

It is evident from these references that the author
of the Epistle of Barnabas believed there was a day in
the future when Christ would return and bring both
physical resurrection and judgment upon all men. Thus
he stands in firm agreement with the rest of the church
fathers we have noted.

### Shepherd of Hermas

As before, the author of this famous work is unknown. The standard date accepted is between A.D. 140 and 154. Though there are some who posit dates such as the mid-80s and late 90s, there are no notable scholars who place it before 70.[14] There is, however, evidence to claim it was definitely written after the book of Revelation (thus for those holding to the view of this book—preterism—this gives even more weight to the Shepherd's testimony).[15]

There are only two references that are helpful in this work, but the first is especially helpful. The first reference is to Judgment Day. The author specifically warns his readers to "Look to the coming judgment" (Hv. 3.9.5). His context is clearly in the realm of a future judgment of all men for their deeds. He is discussing a future judgment he and his readers will participate in, and he hopes to be able to give a good account of them on that day (Hv. 3.9.10).[16]

What is even more significant here though is what word the author uses to refer to the Lord's "coming." By common pantelist interpretation, whenever this word[17] appears in the New Testament (since they view it strictly as a technical term), it is definitely referring to the coming of Christ in the first century. If the Shepherd was writing post-70 and uses the book of Revelation in certain instances, then it is clear the author did not consider this word to be limited in reference to Christ's coming to judge ancient Israel. He obviously believed Christ was going to come again (on some day future to him) to judge the world.

### Why the Confusion of Passages?

At this point it's pertinent to state the reason the early Church made a mistake with regard to certain texts of Scripture. It is evident why the apostles taught both about the coming of Christ in the first century, as well as the Final Advent of Christ to judge all men (not just Israel) at the end of history. It took years, however, for all of the texts of the New Testament to be copied and then circulated among all the churches. During this time it was already believed (based on the verbal teaching of the Apostles) that Christ was to return on some unknown day in the future to judge all men. Thus when the numerous texts of the Scriptures did get into the hands of churches that had not seen some of these texts ever before (probably towards the end of the first century, but definitely after the year 70), they began to misinterpret the texts that refer to the judgment on Israel in 70 as being the same as the texts that refer to the Final Advent of Christ at the end of the world. Clearly, not all of them did this; many plainly did view (correctly) numerous prophecies as relating to Christ's destruction of Jerusalem.[18] If, however, the apostles never taught about a Final Advent, why did the Church misinterpret only some of the texts?

### Conclusion

With the above evidence, it is clear the early Church (late first century to early second century) either forgot the Final Advent had already happened, or were never taught that by the apostles (either through negligence or intent). It is difficult to imagine such an essential doctrine as the Second Coming of Christ could be taught in such a poor fashion that the Church fathers forgot the truth. Hence if they were not taught that the only coming of Christ was to be against Jerusalem in A.D. 70—and we hold to apostolic authority in all doctrine—we are not going to allow that this occurred because of negligence in the apostles' teaching efforts. We have, therefore, only one conclusion: it was their intent not to teach this.

The apostles taught (through their words as well as their writings[19]) that there was a "coming" of Christ other than the one prophesied to come in A.D. 70, which was to be at the end of the world and would include a physical resurrection of all men and an eternal judgment of the same.

Now the question we must ask of the pantelist is: How did the Church forget that the Final Judgment and Resurrection had already occurred, and that there was to be no future coming of Christ (after 70), if the apostles had taught pantelism as clearly as the pantelist urges? In fact, how is it that if the apostles and prophets had never taught that there was going to be a Final Coming of Christ at the end of the world (along with the Resurrection and Judgment), how could those who had supposedly never heard it, so quickly invent such heresy?

*Notes:*

[1] See Gentry, Kenneth, *Before Jerusalem Fell* (San Francisco, CA: Christian Universities Press, 1997) pp. 41–109.

[2] Holmes, Michael, *The Apostolic Fathers* (Grand Rapids, MI: Baker Book House, 1989) p. 25.

[3] See e.g., Leonard and Leonard, *The Promise of His Coming* (Arlington Heights, IL: Laudemont Press, 1996) pp. 161–182; Russell, J. Stuart, *The Parousia* (Bradford, PA: Kingdom Pub., 1996) pp. 199–212.

[4] Holmes, *Apostolic*, pp. 65–67.

[5] He uses τήν μέλλουσαν here. If he believes we do not know the exact day of the "coming" of Christ, then he obviously does not believe this word can only refer to an event that is soon but only that it can do so in certain contexts.

[6] Holmes, *Apostolic*, p. 82.

[7] ἀληθῶs—"truly, in truth, really, actually," Arndt, William F. and Gingrich, F. Wilbur, *A Greek-English Lexicon of the New Testament and Other Early Christian Literature* (Chicago: University of Chicago Press, 1979) p. 37 (hereafter *BAG*).

[8] ὁμοίωμα—"likeness . . . in this way," *BAG*, 567.

[9] Holmes, *Apostolic*, p. 120.

[10] ἐκζητήσει—fut. act. ind.

[11] ἐγερεῖ—fut. act. ind.

[12] It is admitted that Polycarp does not use a future tense in reference to the judgment, but the entire context of living righteously because of standing "before the judgment seat of Christ" in the future would be pointless if Polycarp were speaking of something that was a past event. If it were past he could say: "live how you want, you've already been judged."

[13] Holmes, *Apostolic*, p. 160.

[14] Holmes, *Apostolic*, p. 191.

[15] See Gentry, *Before Jerusalem*, p. 86ff.

[16] Though he speaks of the "coming" or "approaching" (*BAG*, p. 452) judgment, the shepherd does not use any of the standard words that press a preterist interpretation for the reference. He does not use μέλλω, which can denote nearness: "be about to" (*BAG*, p. 501), but rather ἡ ἐπερχομένη, which does not itself denote any nearness but only futurity: "come (on), approach" (*BAG*, p. 285).

[17] παρουσία

[18] See Gentry, *Before Jerusalem*, pp. 68–109.

[19] We know the apostles and prophets of the first century taught verbally and that their verbal teachings were not only helpful for interpreting their writings but also were the background for them. See 1 Thess. 3:4; 2 Thess. 2:5; 2 Pet. 3:2.

# Chapter Two

# The Reign of Christ

ONE PARTICULAR CRITICISM THAT CAN BE RAISED AGAINST THE pantelist position regards the *reign* of Christ. Although there are common references to the lasting nature of His reign (Is. 9:7; Dan. 7:14), Scripture also teaches that Christ's reign is limited in time (e.g., 1 Cor. 15:24 and Rev. 20:1–6). Certainly the lasting nature of the reign must be interpreted within the context of the "limits" Scripture imposes upon it; they cannot contradict each other. When asked if Christ fulfilled His reign in A.D. 70, the pantelist says, "yes, all was fulfilled in 70." When asked, however, whether Christ is still reigning now, the pantelist says, "yes, His reign is eternal." He wants it both ways. The difficulty for the pantelist is that if the reign of Christ described in the Bible is not yet completed in our day, then the things that are said to come at the end of that reign have not yet occurred either.

In the Old Testament, the coming reign of the Messiah shows up more frequently as the history of the nation of Israel progresses. There are certain faint descriptions that we can see clearly only when we look at them from the perspective of their fulfillment.[1] By the time of the prophets, we find that the promises are given more clearly, yet still in a reserved fashion. Let us look first at a few of the prophecies we find that describe the reign of Christ.

> To us a child is born . . . of the increase of his government
> and of peace there will be no end . . . from this time forth and
> for evermore. (Is. 9:6–7)

> David my servant shall be their prince for ever. I will make
> . . . an everlasting covenant with them . . . and I will set
> my sanctuary in the midst of them forevermore.
> (Ezek. 37:25–26)

> There came one like a son of man . . . and to him was given
> dominion and glory and kingdom . . . [and] his dominion is
> an everlasting dominion, which shall not pass away, and his
> kingdom one that shall not be destroyed. (Dan. 7:13–14)

There are many passages which could be quoted in this regard, yet I will limit it to these for the present. Each of these three passages shows how the Messiah's reign was clearly to have "no end." The point rings true in these (and numerous other) passages that the Messiah's kingdom is to remain "forevermore."

When we come to the New Testament, we find the fulfillment of these prophesies in the person of Jesus Christ. He is the "child" in Isaiah, the "David" in Ezekiel, and the "son of man" in Daniel. One of the clearest allusions to the passages cited above is found in Luke. At the Annunciation, the angel tells Mary:

> He will be great, and will be called the Son of the Most High;
> and the Lord God will give to him the throne of his father
> David, and he will reign over the house of Jacob forever; and
> of his kingdom there will be no end. (Luke 1:32–33)

We can see from this the continuation of the idea of the eternal nature of the Messiah's kingdom. What can be drawn from this text? It essentially says four things: first, Christ will be recognized as more than a mere man ("Son of the Most High"); second, He will fulfill the promises to David; third, He will be the head of "Jacob" (the Church); and fourth, His kingdom will be eternal. This is not a point of contention between the preterist and the pantelist, but it must be stated before we proceed.

Let us now examine some of the details the New Testament gives about the kingdom. There are two statements made by Paul in Corinthians which cause a certain degree of confusion on the eternal status of the kingdom. The statements are as follows:

> Then comes the end, when He delivers the kingdom to God the Father.... When all things are subject to Him, then the Son Himself will also be subject to Him who put all things under Him. (1 Cor. 15:24, 28)

The fact that causes a bit of confusion in these verses is that Christ is said to "deliver the kingdom" over and that He too will be "subjected" to the Father. The delivering of the kingdom does not do anything to specifically negate the eternity of the kingdom (the kingdom is not "ended," it is "handed over"). It does, however, point to a specific change in the kingdom. The change with regard to the ruler of the kingdom at first may cause us to take notice of how this seems to go against what is said elsewhere regarding Christ's eternal reign.[2] The mention of Christ being "subjected" to the Father should also make us curious as to the effect this has on this glorious truth.

Let us step back and examine for a moment what we know of the office of Christ. We know that at the Son's birth as a man He took on a position He never had before; "for a little while [He] was made lower than the angels" (Heb. 2:9), and He "emptied himself, taking the form of a servant, being born in the likeness of men" (Phil. 2:7). After His death and resurrection, He was *given* "all authority in heaven and on earth" by the Father (Matt. 28:18). He has all things *put* in "subjection under Him" by the Father (1 Cor. 15:27), and the Father *"made him* sit at His right hand" (Eph. 1:20; emphasis added).

If we are merely considering the divinity of Christ these statements will cause severe difficulty for us.[3] In His divinity He was always God and thus is always in full sovereignty. One does not give to God authority He already has. If, however, we consider that the second person of the Trinity willingly took an inferior position while on earth[4] and subsequently (at His exaltation) was given the position of full sovereignty in everything, this causes little trouble for us. Christ, as the "God-man," is temporarily given a position that He did not have before He was incarnated.[5] Before His incarnation He was the second person of the Trinity; after His exaltation, He takes the special position of Lord of the universe that was previously held by the Trinity as a whole. He holds this position now because He is bringing the kingdom to this world and returning it to its original design (which we perverted at the fall in Adam).

I am speaking here of the difference between the "natural" dominion Christ holds as God and the "economic" dominion He has as the specially appointed mediator between God the Father and man.[6] Similar to this is the idea that the Holy Spirit is fully God and deserving of all glory and honor, but for the present (in the "economic" position He holds) His responsibility is to give all glory to the Son (John 16:14).[7]

This does not in any way mean that the Father and the Spirit no longer have any authority; they have authority by nature as God. The issue is that if the Son also has authority by nature as God, how would He be given "all authority"? He can only be "given all authority" if the Father and the Spirit choose to allow Christ to act as the vice-regent of the Godhead, temporarily, in order to be the human (and divine) head of the Church until she reaches full redemption and is completely free from all of the effects of the fall. God the Father and

the Spirit always have sovereignty; they have just chosen God the Son (in His resurrected incarnate form)
to act with "all authority in heaven and on earth."

Where does all this get us? Back in 1 Corinthians
Paul said that someday in the future Christ would hand
over the kingdom to the first person of the Trinity and
would surrender His position as vice-regent and
subject Himself to the Father: "Then comes the end,
when he delivers the kingdom to God the Father"
(1 Cor. 15:24).[8]

Thus His special position as the absolute, sovereign,
mediating God-man is only temporary, while His divine sovereignty as the second person of the Trinity is
eternal. After He finishes making all of His enemies
His footstool, He will no longer need to be "seated at
the right hand of God the Father" because that is His
position as vice-regent. Sitting at the right hand of God
is not a description of His divinity but of His special
and temporary position of redeemer of this fallen world.[9]
If Christ did not hold a special position as vice-regent,
then He would not be able to give up that position and
"be subjected to Him who put all things under Him"
(1 Cor. 15:28). Why does Christ need to return to His
prior position and surrender the kingdom to the Father? Paul himself answers this question when he says
that it is so that "God may be all in all" (1 Cor. 15:28
NAS). The Trinity must return to its "pre-creation"
order and give up its "administrative hierarchy," once
the purpose of that hierarchy has finished.

As Turretin said, Christ will always remain the head
of the Church, but "the work of salvation having been
consummated," He will "deliver up the kingdom, not
by a deposition and abdication of it, but by an exhibi-
tion of it as consummated [and] will return it to God,
who had delivered it to" Him.[10] On that glorious day,
Christ, the absolute sovereign, will stand before the
Father and say, to the fullest extent possible, "Here is

the kingdom that you gave me to rule over, I have accomplished 'the work you gave me to do'" (John 17:4
NIV).

## Christ Represents God

Helpful to this idea of Christ's special position are two
other passages in 1 Corinthians. Paul's concept of Christ
handing over the kingdom to the Father is easily connected with other things Paul says within the same letter. In 3:23, Paul has just finished telling his readers
how all Christians are united in their work for the Lord
and that God will judge the work of each on "that Day"
(3:13). In rebuking those who said they "belong to Paul"
(1:12), Paul points out how every Christian be-
longs to Christ: "you are Christ's" (3:23). The context
(3:21–22) shows that Paul is also speaking of the
Christian's authority over the world. Thus Paul is saying, "We all work together as we strive to bring the
kingdom of God to this world, so don't judge the work
that God has another Christian doing. In bringing the
kingdom to this world you [as the body of Christ—
3:16] represent Christ." His next statement is what we
are aiming at: "and Christ is God's" (3:23). What does
he mean by this? Our text is clear; as we represent Christ
here on earth in bringing in the kingdom, so Christ (as
vice-regent) represents the triune God as sovereign over
the kingdom.

One other passage is helpful in this regard. Paul, in
discussing how man was made to be the authority in
the family and how the wife is given as his helper, says
that "the head of every man is Christ, the head of a
woman is her husband, and the head of Christ is God"
(1 Cor. 11:3). Man is the "image and glory of God; but
woman is the glory of man" (11:7). Here the same truth
as above is represented in a different fashion. Woman
represents man (specifically her husband) and acts as
his helper, man represents Christ and acts as His

"helper," while Christ represents God and acts as His "Helper." Paul said "the head of Christ is God" because, in developing this idea of Christ's vice-regency, he is making it clear that Christ is working in a special position for the present time. Thus when we arrive at 15:24ff, we need to recognize that Paul has already laid the groundwork for this idea that Christ will deliver the kingdom to the Father and a change in rulership will occur.

Other New Testament statements verify this truth as well. This is why we find Christ referring to the Father as "my God" (Matt. 27:46, John 20:17, Rev. 3:12). We also see Christ's intercession for us needing to continue throughout this age because we still sin after A.D. 70 (we have not been glorified yet; see 1 Jn. 2:1). Paul even specifically connects Christ's intercession for us with His sitting at the right hand of God (which we know is temporary). In Romans 8:34, Paul says, "Christ Jesus . . . who is at the right hand of God, who indeed intercedes for us."[11] Finally, here we can note the praise that is given to the Son in Revelation. In His special position as vice-regent (as a result of His sacrificial death), He is depicted as the only one worthy to open the scroll (Rev. 5:5). The praise showered on Christ in this context is primarily focused on His special mediatorial position (seen in reference to the "Lamb"), and His association with the Father shows that His vice-regency is also referred to here (5:12–13).

## The Length of the Vice-regency

Now consider this glorious truth in relation to two other statements in the New Testament that will help us to see the duration Christ's vice-regency has.

> [He] made him sit at his right hand in the heavenly places, far above all rule and authority and power and dominion, and above every name that is named, not only in this age but also in *that which is to come.* (Eph. 1:20–21; emphasis added)

> For it was not to angels that God subjected *the world to come.*
> (Heb. 2:5; emphasis added)

It is obvious that for both Paul and the author of Hebrews, their "age to come" is the age in which we live now; they were alive at the end of the Jewish age, and we now live in the Messianic age.[12] In addition, both Paul and the author of Hebrews affirm that in our age Christ will still have His special position of vice-regent over all. They portray the special subjection of all things as extending beyond the time between the resurrection of Christ and the destruction of Jerusalem. Once again, these verses are not referring to the natural subjection of all things to Christ as God, because that subjection does not need to be brought about by the Father; it is intrinsic to creation itself to be subject to the sovereign Lord of all. These two passages are speaking about the special subjection of all things that the Father brought about after Christ "came to the ancient of Days and was presented before him" so He could give Him "dominion and glory and kingdom, that all people, nations, and languages should serve him" (Dan. 7:13–14).

In Ephesians, Paul is clearly referring to both Psalm 8:4–6 and Psalm 110:1. The author of Hebrews goes so far as to quote Psalm 8:4–6 in Hebrews 2:6–8, while referring to Psalm 110:1 in other places (see Heb. 1:3, 13; 8:1; 10:12; 12:2). They both believed Christ would continue to hold his special position in our age. Once again, they are obviously referring to His vice-regency because of their use of the standard ideas related to it: all things being subjected under him by the Father, sitting at the right hand of the Father, having all authority and power (as opposed to sharing it with the Father and the Spirit). Thus He would not have handed it over yet, in our present age, to God the Father until "after destroying every rule and every authority and power" (1 Cor. 15:24).

If, therefore, Christ is still seated at the right hand of the Father and is there ruling as the Father's vice-regent, then according to Paul's understanding of the kingdom, the "coming" of Christ to resurrect His own, the "end" and the destruction of the "last enemy" (death), has not yet come (and it is clear from the context that Paul refers to the destruction of death as occurring at our resurrection). Consequently, we are still waiting for these events to occur (1 Cor. 15:23–26). There is no other understanding of this passage available to us. Either Christ is still in His special position of vice-regent over the kingdom of God (and thus pantelism cannot stand), or Christ has finished His vice-regency and the "age to come" which Paul spoke of has already come and gone.[13]

The dispensationalists are bad enough when they limit the glorious Messianic age to a mere thousand years; the pantelists have limited it to a mere forty years. In trying to avoid errors like those found in dispensationalism, the pantelists have found a new way to reduce the glory of Christ even further than dispensationalism. The terms used in the Scriptures to describe the reign of Christ as vice-regent can in no way fit within a forty-year period; they describe an enduring period of time that spans numerous generations, not the one generation of A.D. 30–70.

Thus Christ is still on His throne, He still has "all authority in heaven and on earth," and He has not yet finished the task He willingly undertook to accomplish for the glory of God: the full destruction of all His enemies, the end of this age, and the resurrection of all those who are His.

## Why Such a Long Vice-regency?

There are two main reasons for such an extended vice-regency. First, we see that Christ, as our husband, is working to sanctify us (Eph. 5:26). Though we have

come to maturity such that we can be married to Christ
(Eph. 4:13), we are still covered with blemishes that
He needs to remove (Eph. 5:27). This is the reason the
marriage feast continues now, and we await the full con-
summation of our union with Christ; He is still "wash-
ing [us] with the word" (Eph. 5:26) that He might
present us to Himself "in glorious splendor" (Eph. 5:27).
The Church is clearly still in need of sanctifying in many
areas, and unless the pantelist wants to say that the lack
of doctrinal and practical unity that exists today is something that needs no improvement, they too must admit
we are not yet "holy and without blemish" (Eph. 5:27).
We indeed have a long way to go while Christ puts His
enemies under His feet.[14]

The second reason is connected to the first. At the
cross, Christ already had everything put under His feet
(1 Cor. 15:27), yet He still "must reign until he has
put all his enemies under his feet" (1 Cor. 15:25). What
is Paul referring to here? Though Christ fully won the
battle on the cross two thousand years ago, He was told
by the Father to "rule in the midst of your foes!"
(Ps. 110:2). Thus He is allowing His enemies to shake
their fists at Him (using them for the purpose of purifying and perfecting His bride) until He has made each
of them visibly admit He is Lord of all by bowing their
knees to Him and therefore bringing glory to the Father (Phil. 2:10–11). The last enemy He will make bow
to Him is physical death. He conquered it on the cross
(Acts 2:24), but it too is allowed to continue to kick
and scream until its final end (1 Cor. 15:25–26,
51–55). In the meantime Christ holds "death" on a short
leash (see Rev. 1:18).

Christ, our Sovereign, is presently still seated at the
right hand of God the Father. He will remain there
ruling for the Father until He has perfected His bride
and destroyed all of His and her enemies. At that time
He will hand over the special possession of the king-

dom to the Father to glorify Him above all. The Son will then give up His special vice-regency and call His bride to Himself to consummate their marriage, and He will live for eternity with her in joyous union.

## Universal Blessing

Going even beyond the above discussion, yet another piece of pantelism doesn't fit into the context of the reign of Christ. If all prophecies were fulfilled by A.D. 70, then it should be impossible to find a prophecy that refers to anything that had not occurred by A.D. 70. If, however, there are references to things that come after A.D. 70, then pantelism is false at the very heart of its assertions. The clearest event described in Scripture that points to a time beyond the destruction of Jerusalem (outside of the Judgment, the Resurrection and the Final Advent as seen in chapters four, five, and six) is the universal blessing that comes to the world as a result of the gospel. Whether one follows the dispensational lead and places this period of blessing after the Second Coming, or the postmillennial vision which places these blessings before, such passages don't fit into a pantelist framework without implausible twisting. Let us examine a few passages in this regard.

### Psalm 72

In the Psalms we find some of the most beautiful descriptions of the Messianic age in all of Scripture. Psalm 72, originally used in reference to the ancient kings of Israel, has clear application to the reign of Christ. The prayer for the "ultimate" king of Israel was that He would not only have "dominion from sea to sea, and from the River to the ends of the earth" (72:8), but also that "all kings" would "fall down before him" (72:11). This clearly did not happen to any of the kings of ancient Israel; it is only fulfilled in the reign of our Lord and Savior Jesus Christ. He is the true "King of kings."

Yet we must ask here, did "all kings fall down before Him" in A.D. 70?

If this then is a prophecy of nations of Gentiles bowing down before Christ, can we say that the "kings" of the Gentile nations bowed down before Christ in A.D. 70? The common pantelist response is to say "if the Bible says they did, then they did." Yes, if the Bible said they did, then they did. The problem is neither this text nor the others say that this event took place in the first century destruction of Jerusalem. There is in fact no time reference given in any of these texts that prophesy the subjugation of the Gentile nations.

Did the emperor of Rome (Vespasian) bow before Christ in 70? No. If we wish to consider "falling down before" Christ as professing His lordship, that did not happen to a (living) Roman emperor until the fourth century. If we consider "falling down before" Christ as being destroyed (as Israel was in 70), then that did not happen for another century after Constantine. In addition there were many nations and kings that had not even come into existence in 70 that were (and are) yet to bow before Christ. This prophecy clearly refers to the submission of numerous Gentiles to Christ, an event still happening today and will continue to happen for as long as this earth remains (probably thousands of years). This truth, in and of itself, negates the basic assumption of pantelism.

### Isaiah 2
Isaiah also has numerous prophecies of the Messianic age that relate to what we are discussing here. In chapter two of Isaiah, we find the glorious prophecy of how Christ brought the Messianic kingdom to the people of God. In 2:4 we read:

> He shall judge between the nations, and shall decide for many peoples; and they shall beat their swords into plowshares, and their spears into pruning hooks; nation shall not

lift up sword against nation, neither shall they learn war any
more.

This prophecy is usually either spiritualized away to
refer to the peace which Christ brings to the individual
believer (as in Rom. 5:1), or it is projected into the
future "reign" of Christ in a conjectured millennium
(by the dispensationalists). Postmillennialists have long
seen this passage (and others like it) as referring to the
successful influence of the gospel throughout the world.
This description of the glorious kingdom, over which
Christ reigns today, tells of a wondrous day in which
there is no longer "war any more."

The confidence we have that Christ will bring about
that day does not waver at all because we "do not yet
see everything in subjection to him" (Heb. 2:8). The
pantelist also has a confidence of the truthfulness of
this passage. There is nothing in Isaiah 2:1–4 that necessitates that the universal peace will occur instanta-
neously at the time of the "mountain of the house of
the Lord" being established (which did occur at the time
Israel was destroyed in A.D. 70). The Scriptures actually refer to the reign of Christ more as a process that
extends over a long period of time than as a quick event
that accomplishes everything in an instant.[15]

This idea of a process is also seen in Matthew 25
(where the first part of Isaiah 2:4 is clearly alluded to).
We read that when (or after) Christ sits down on His
glorious throne "before him will be gathered all the
nations, and he will separate them one from another"
(25:32). This is evidently not an event that took place
in A.D. 70. Although at that time Christ did gather the
nation of Israel before Him and brought punishment
upon them, He did not at that time judge "all the nations."

## Daniel 2

One of Daniel's most well known prophecies refers to the coming of the kingdom of God to destroy the Roman empire. In chapter two, Daniel interprets the dream Nebuchadnezzar has of the four-part statue (2:31–35). Daniel says there are four kingdoms represented in the statue: Babylon, Persia, Greece, and Rome. The conclusion of the dream was that God would destroy those kingdoms by the coming of a spiritual kingdom (one "cut out by no human hand," 2:34).

The timing of the coming of the spiritual kingdom of God is given very clearly with the phrase "in the days of those kings" of the fourth kingdom of Rome (2:44). Even though it is said that the kingdom of God will destroy "all these kingdoms" (all four listed above, 2:44), we are specifically told that the kingdom to be specifically struck by the kingdom of God is Rome ("it smote the image on its feet," 2:34), thus limiting the timing of the actual coming to the time of Rome. As above we ask, when did the Roman empire fall? Not in A.D. 70 but almost four hundred years later. Although the kingdom of Christ came fully in the first century, it was not until four centuries later that Rome fell. We have here another fulfilled prophecy of an event that occured after A.D. 70. This conversion of Rome took centuries.

In addition, there is more said in Daniel than merely the subjugation of Rome. We are told that "all dominions shall serve and obey" the saints (7:27). This "serving and obeying" is something that has not fully come to pass. Yes, we acknowledge that there are numerous "dominions" that have been subjected to the kingdom of God, but there are dominions today not subject to Him, as well as dominions yet to be. This too, clearly refers to a process that goes on throughout the Messianic age. Today, America is by no means "serving and obeying" the saints (in spite of the many opportunities she has had). Some day, though, America will bow before Christ. This will either happen through her destruction (as with Israel of the first century) or through conversion (as with the Romans). Let us pray it is the latter.

*Notes:*
[1] E.g., Genesis 49:10, Numbers 24:17, Deuteronomy 18:15; for my perspective of understanding these verses better after the cross, see Ephesians 3:5.

[2] Turretin, Francis, *Institutes of Elenctic Theology*. (Philippsburg, NJ: Presbyterian and Reformed Publ., 1992) 13.19.13.

[3] As with Matthew 24:36 and Christ's lack of knowledge about the day He was to return.

[4] This is the reason why the cults deny the divinity of Christ. They emphasize the passages which speak of His human qualities at the expense of the passages which clearly show His divinity.

[5] Turretin, *Institutes,* 13.19.12.

[6] Ibid., 3.22.3.

[7] Similar to note four, many cults deny the divinity of the Spirit because they emphasize the temporary "economic" position the Spirit takes, as though it were a universal situation that always has been and always will be.

[8] Turretin considers the subjection of Christ to possibly be referring to His humanity returning the ("borrowed") authority to the trinity, *Institutes*, 14.17.11. This is similar to the twenty-four Elders casting their "crowns" (symbolizing divinely bestowed authority) before the Lord in Revelation 4:10.

[9] There is really nothing wrong with limiting the reign of Christ to a period of time. Both the Jewish sabbath and the Levitical priesthood were described as perpetual (Ex. 31:13–17 and 40: 14–15), yet they definitely ended in the first century. Their perpetuity was obviously limited to the age in which they were applicable. Likewise Christ's reign is perpetual during this age (and will end when this age does). For more on this idea see: Owen, John, *An Exposition of the Epistle to the Hebrews* (Carlisle, PA: Banner of Truth Trust, 1991), vol. 5, p. 490.

[10] Turretin, *Institutes,* 14.17.10.

[11] In fact, in the pantelist scheme of things, since sinful men will continue on earth forever, Christ could never cease to sit at the right hand of God because He would have to be interceding for Christians for all eternity. He would never be able to complete the work that He started.

[12] Which, interestingly enough, is always referred to as an "age," which automatically connotes a beginning *and* an end! The "age to come" is never referred to as eternal because "ages" have a beginning and an end.

[13] If the pantelists wish to opt for this idea they will need to come up with a theologically and historically significant event (with biblical support) that would have been the point at which Paul's "age to come" ended and our age began. The "age to come" cannot have ended in A.D. 70, that is when it began. Pantelism has made the New Testament understanding of the reign of Christ not only absurd but also impossible to reconcile with itself.

[14] By definition the pantelist admits that the Church has theological error: he disagrees with the majority of the Church about eschatology. Therefore he must admit that there are (at least) theological enemies that Christ has not yet put under His feet.

[15] See Ps. 110:1 "Sit at my right hand" (take a place of vice-regency), *"till"* (for an unspecified period of time), "I make your enemies your footstool" (*all* enemies are subjected). This extended period of time is also assumed in verse 2; that Christ is told to "Rule in the midst of [His] foes" assumes that not all His enemies are subjected at the beginning of the "rule" but as a process over time.

# Chapter Three

# Bondage to Decay

ACCORDING TO PANTELIST INTERPRETATIONS, THIS physical world we live on will go on forever; history will never end. We cannot say this is impossible for God to do; He can do anything He wants. The question we must ask is whether this is scriptural testimony. Admittedly, the Scriptures portray the end of the Jewish age by terms that describe the dissolution of the cosmos at large. That does not mean, however, every time we see a reference to the world ending that we are to automatically interpret it as being symbolic of the Jewish age. If the Scriptures do say that this world we live on will not continue forever, then we are bound to believe it. Just what does the Bible say about this physical world?

Modern "doom and gloom" prophets have so filled our minds with their lies that it is almost impossible to imagine that the world we live in won't be destroyed within a few years. Whether it be the result of a (supposed) new hole in the ozone or World War III (which of course will be started by the "Antichrist"), the majority opinion is clearly that we don't have long to go. An orthodox examination of the Scriptures would lead one to see this is not necessarily so. In fact we may have thousands of years to go before the Final Advent.[1] Dispensationalists would consider this to be radically unscriptural. They view all the "soon" passages (which actually prove preterism and disprove dispensationalism) to mean that we should always have an "imminent" expectation of the Final Advent—even though a coming that is "always soon" ends up being meaningless (because "always soon" means "never soon").

Saying the world will probably be here for a few thousand more years does not, however, negate the fact that this earth is fallen. When Adam fell, mankind was not the only thing affected. The rest of creation was also affected:

> And to Adam he said, "Because you have listened to the voice of your wife, and have eaten of the tree of which I commanded you, 'You shall not eat of it,' cursed is the ground *because of you*; in toil you shall eat of it all the days of your life; thorns and thistles it shall bring forth to you." (Gen. 3:17–18; emphasis added)

The ground (or the earth) also fell with man. The specific description by Moses is that the ground was "cursed." This same word is used in Genesis 3:14 to refer to the condemnation of Satan, in 4:11 to refer to Cain after he murdered Abel, and in 5:29 to refer once again to the ground "which the Lord has cursed." In each of these instances the word is used to emphasize that God cursed the things in question.

The earth's being cursed brought it into a state unlike what it was in before. God specifically says it is going to have "thorns and thistles" and that man will need to "toil" to be successful in working the ground. Originally the earth was to be the place where man was to live in safety (Gen. 2:8), and man was to care for the earth (Gen. 2:5). After the fall, however, man was no longer simply the caretaker of the earth, he was also its victim. He would have to labor and toil to get the earth to help him survive. One of the original purposes for nonhuman creation was that it was to be cared for by man; after the fall it fought against Adam and had to be subdued by him.

Not only did creation become man's "opponent," it also began to experience death. Plants and animals became subject to disease and death. The very existence of "sub-human" creation had become futile. It was supposed to last forever and had a purpose to fulfill, but now its very existence was defeating that purpose.[2] The curse upon the earth still remains and has not been lifted. Even after the resurrection of Christ, animals and trees (as well as mankind) still die.

Likewise the curses that were put upon Eve (Gen. 3:16) and Adam (Gen. 3:17–18) are still in effect. The curses have not (yet) been removed by the crucifixion and resurrection of Christ. Christian women still experience suffering in childbirth, and Christian men still labor in order to "eat of the land." Does this mean Christ was unable to redeem man from these things? It is obvious He is able; He has just *not yet* done so. According to pantelism, Christ did not and never will redeem mankind from the primary curses of the fall. Humanity must endure these things forever. Yes, pantelists acknowledge that upon death man will no longer experience these things, because he will then be apart from this "mortal body." It is an incredible insult to Christ's work on the cross to say the curses of the fall will never be completely done away with. (Remember, according to pantelism the present creation goes on forever; thus it is never redeemed.)

Even pantelists should see that this is a pitiful reduction of the redemption brought by Christ. This makes Christ able to save our souls but unable to reverse the curses put upon our bodies or the curse put upon the earth. The glorious "eternal kingdom" (2 Pet. 1:11) will forever have pain and toil, while we stand back and watch the physical creation continue to decay. Just how long can the physical creation withstand the sinful manner in which men treat it? This unredeemed earth cannot last for eternity unless God does something to it and removes the "curse" from it. It will certainly last longer than the environmentalists say it will, but another six thousand years does not compare to eternity.

The foolishness of denying the fullness of biblical redemption goes beyond this though. Paul picks up on this concept in Romans 8 and thus helps us to see more of the pantelist error. Let us look at the passage in full:

> [18] I consider that the sufferings of this present time are not worth comparing with the glory that is to be revealed to us. [19] For the creation waits with eager longing for the revealing of the sons of God; [20] for the creation was subjected to futility, not of its own will but by the will of him who subjected it in hope; [21] because the creation itself will be set free from its bondage to decay and obtain the glorious liberty of the children of God. [22] We know that the whole creation has been groaning in travail together until now; [23] and not only the creation, but we ourselves, who have the first fruits of the Spirit, groan inwardly as we wait for adoption as sons, the redemption of our bodies. [24] For in this hope we were saved. Now hope that is seen is not hope. For who hopes for what he sees? [25] But if we hope for what we do not see, we wait for it with patience. (Rom. 8:18–25)

It should be clear to all that Paul is discussing here the same thing I discussed above—the fall of both mankind and creation and the hope for redemption from that fall. (In addition, the similarity this passage has with 2 Corinthians 4:14–5:10 ["momentary affliction"] should be evident.) Let me now examine Romans 8:18–25 verse by verse:

*8:18—I consider that the sufferings of this present time are not worth comparing with the glory that is to be revealed to us.* The similarity this verse has with 2 Corinthians 4:17 is clear. Paul is discussing how suffering means nothing when compared with the glory to come.

He contrasts the suffering of the "present time" with
the future "glory." This suffering cannot be our suffering under the sinfulness of the flesh. Although Paul
refers to sin in 8:9–13, he makes our suffering necessary for our receiving glory in verse seventeen.[3] Sin may
be inevitable in this world, but it is not "necessary" for
our glory. Some have claimed that the "glory that is to
be revealed" should be rendered "about to be revealed"
because of the Greek word used there. This word is
not, however, a technical term that always carries this
connotation. In fact, in this instance, "about to be" causes
more confusion in the text, as will be seen below. Next
we must ask, is this time of suffering over? There is
nothing in this verse or within the context of the entire
chapter to say that Paul was speaking of a particular
suffering under the Jews of the first century. Nothing
within this passage limits the suffering to a particular
time, other than that the suffering will end when the
"glory is . . . revealed," and the time for the revealing
of the "glory" is left open.

*8:19—For the creation waits with eager longing for
the revealing of the sons of God.* Creation is said to "wait"
for the revealing of the sons of God. The reference
personifies the earth (and probably the animals also).
It cannot be referring to the "new creation" that came
at the cross, for it was already present (2 Cor. 5:17).[4]
What is the "revealing" creation is waiting for? This
must be something more than what already existed for
Christians in Paul's day (e.g., Rom. 9:6–8; Gal. 3:25–29),
for it was already clear that only those who truly believed in Christ were the "sons of God." This "revealing" must therefore go beyond that. One can see a strong
connection between what Paul says here and what John
says in 1 John 3:2—"we are God's children now; it does
not yet appear what we shall be, but we know that when
he appears we shall be like him, for we shall see him as

he is." John, like Paul, says that we are already God's children, but something yet to happen will make us even more so. This also connects with the past adoption in Romans 8:15 (we are "God's children now"—1 Jn. 3:2) and its difference from the future adoption in Romans 8:23 (we don't yet know "what we shall be"—1 Jn. 3:2).

*8:20—for the creation was subjected to futility, not of its own will but by the will of him who subjected it in hope.* Here Paul explains what happened when God "subjected it in hope." It was subjected in hope so that someday it would be delivered from that subjection (v. 21). The word Paul uses to refer to the subjection specifically points to the fall and how God brought about the subjection.[5] This shows how God had, from the beginning, a goal of bringing physical creation out of its state of "futility." He planned to redeem it from the start. If, however, Paul is here speaking of the "old creation" that was done away with in the first century, what is the situation he is discussing? When were the old heavens and earth "subjected to futility" by God? The "heaven and earth" of Judaism that passed away in the first century (2 Pet. 3:10; Rev. 21:1) were "obsolete and growing old" (Heb. 8:13); they were not "futile." How could any Christian consider the Old Covenant that "came with glory" (2 Cor. 3:7) to be futile? Was it futile for God to create the Old Covenant? Did God design a system for the people of God that was futile? We acknowledge that the New far surpasses the Old in glory (2 Cor. 3:10), but that does not make the Old futile. In fact when we compare the Old with the New, it is only now *after* the New has fully come that the Old is considered to be futile. Before the New Covenant had fully come the Old was passing away, but it was *not yet* futile. Consequently the old creation (of the Judaic system) was not delivered *from* futility in A.D. 70, it was delivered *to* futility.

*8:21—because the creation itself will be set free from its bondage to decay and obtain the glorious liberty of the children of God.* This verse shows us specifically what the hope was that God had when He subjected creation "to futility." He "hoped" it would be some day "set free" from its bondage and share in the "liberty of the children of God." The Resurrection is often reworked by the pantelist to mean a spiritual event in which man was delivered from the deadness of his sin to the new life of righteousness. Preterism does not deny that the Scriptures use "life and death" to refer to this truth. It just denies that every time the Bible talks about "life and death" it is referring to a spiritual change; this verse is one of the reasons why. The physical creation Paul is speaking of has neither a spirit (to be changed) nor sin (to be delivered from). Paul is showing here that when the physical bodies of saints are set free from their "bondage to decay," the same will occur for creation. Since creation was subjected as a result of man's sin, it will be delivered as a result of man's deliverance.

The term "bondage to decay"[6] is also indicative of what Paul is speaking of here. The primary meaning of the word "decay" is destruction or corruption. The verb form of the word carries the connotation of "to bring moral corruption" (as in 1 Cor. 3:17 and 2 Cor. 11:3). As mentioned above, Paul cannot be referring to a moral quality, but is rather speaking of the physical corruption that came to the earth at the fall. In fact, Paul uses both the noun and verb in 1 Corinthians 15 to refer to our physical bodies that must be done away with at our resurrection, as well as the negative form of the word (translated as "imperishable" in RSV, NAS, and NIV)[7] to refer to the future resurrection body (see 1 Cor. 15:42, 50, 52, 53, 54). We can see from this that in Romans 8 he is connecting our resurrection with the renewal of the physical earth. In addition, in 1 Corinthians 15, Paul equates "imperishable" with "immortality" (15:53–54).[8] The pantelist is hard-pressed to show how the physical earth can go through a spiritual renewal. Furthermore, if the physical earth's renewal is connected with our resurrection, that too must be physical.

I acknowledge that the pantelist may still want to apply this text to the old "heavens and earth" that was replaced in the first century. We find in this verse, however, a reason this is plainly impossible. Paul does not say here that the present creation will some day be annihilated and be replaced by another creation. He says it will someday be "set free from its bondage." In other words, physical creation is going to be regenerated and brought to new life. When man is born again, he does not have his old spirit destroyed and replaced with another spirit; he has his spirit regenerated. In the Resurrection, man's body will not be destroyed but rather "changed" (1 Cor. 15:51). Likewise the physical creation will not be destroyed but "changed" when it is "set free from its bondage." The image of replacing the Old Heavens and Earth with a New Heavens and Earth occurs in connection with what happened in the first century when the New Covenant replaced the Old. The Old Covenant was "destroyed" and replaced by the New Covenant. The two are related and are similar, but the New is not the Old merely renewed (see Jer. 31:31–32; Rom. 7:6; 2 Cor. 3:3–11; Heb. 7:12). Paul here in Romans 8:21 says the creation "will be set free," not replaced. "Changed into something different" and "replaced by another" are not the same thing. As Psalm 102 says, the physical earth will not last forever, and if it were left without being "set free from its bondage," (Rom. 8:21) it would eventually perish as would man; only God is truly eternal (Ps. 102:25–27).

*8:22—We know that the whole creation has been groaning in travail together until now.* Paul refers here to something that was common, universal knowledge for his readers, not something that had to be revealed by God. The renewal of the spiritual "heavens and earth" that needed to take place was an essential part of the gospel (Mark 1:15). It was so revolutionary that numerous Jews rejected it and were destroyed as a result (Matt. 21:41–43). The "decay" the physical earth experiences is, however, obvious to all. The personification of the creation is a telling illustration of the need for its redemption. The interesting point we notice here is that Paul views the creation as "groaning . . . until now." In his day, the creation had not yet experienced its renewal. As mentioned before, 2 Corinthians 5:17 portrays the New Creation as already come. Paul is here speaking of something different from what he refers to in 2 Corinthians 5:17. The "new creation" that came at the cross was a past event for Paul. He did not look forward to it: the renewal of the physical creation was a future event for him, as it is for us.[9]

8:23—*and not only the creation, but we ourselves, who have the first fruits of the Spirit, groan inwardly as we wait for adoption as sons, the redemption of our bodies.* The weightiness of this verse will keep us in it longer than the others. The first point Paul makes is that it is not only the creation which groans in desire for release. We as Christians want to be released as well. If creation desires its release from physical decay (since it has no spiritual decay), then we must be desiring something of the same nature. We as Christians have been delivered from the dominion of sin already (Rom. 6:2–4); therefore, our "groaning" must be along the lines of the physical corruption and mortality from which we have not yet been delivered.[10] If Paul were saying here that we "groaned" to be delivered from our sin, he would be blatantly contradicting what he has already said in 6:5–23. We have been (past tense) "set free from sin."

Paul here further defines who it is that groans: "we
. . . who have the first fruits of the Spirit." In this there
is no shortage of interpretations for what the "first fruits"
specifically refers to. The word for "first fruits"[11] specifically has the connotation of the first part of the crop,
the quality of which guarantees the latter part of the
crop. Thus if the Spirit has been given in a "first fruit"
sense at conversion, what does Paul want to say is being "guaranteed" of the Spirit in the future? If the pantelist is right, then at A.D. 70 the "rest of the crop" of
the Spirit came to the Church. This, however, cannot
be proven either from history or Scripture. What is different about our experience of the Spirit that is "fuller"
or "better" than what the Christian of the first century
experienced? Nothing, because we too have the "first
fruits" of the Spirit. Thus the "guaranteed" factor of
the Spirit is His further work in resurrecting us from
physical death. This is especially apparent when we
compare Paul's words in Romans 8:11: "he who raised
Christ Jesus from the dead will give life to your mortal
bodies also through his Spirit which dwells in you." Paul's
description of "mortal bodies"[12] in connection with
Christ's resurrection can only refer to our physical
bodies which are subject to death. The Spirit was central in applying the work of Christ to us in our spiritual
conversion, and He will also be central in our physical
resurrection (see 8:10 where Paul says our bodies are
figuratively "dead because of sin" and our "spirits are
alive because of righteousness").

Pantelists claim that placing thousands of years between the "first fruits" and the rest of the "crop" makes
the analogy senseless, since the actual "first fruit" came
(at the most) days or weeks before the rest of the crop.
The pantelist says that forty years (from A.D. 30 to 70)
doesn't stretch the "first fruit" concept. If any farmer
were told he had to wait forty years for the rest of his
crop, he would consider that ridiculous. Obviously the

length of time is not the issue (even if Jesus was referring to a forty-year time span, He knew that forty years
was a ludicrous amount of time for crops). The issue is
that the "first fruit" is a guarantee of the rest of the
crop, however long one must wait for it to come.

   This concept of the Spirit's presence now being a
"first fruit" of what He will do in the future is virtually
equivalent to Paul's concept of the Spirit as a "down
payment."[13] In 2 Corinthians 5:5, after Paul has said,
"He who raised the Lord Jesus will raise us also" (4:14),
he speaks of how the Christian "groans" (5:4 NAS) because he wants to be "further clothed"[14] by having his
"mortal" body "swallowed up by life" (5:4). What has
God done as a guarantee of this event? He "has given
us the Spirit as a guarantee" (5:5). We see Paul here
using the Spirit's presence in the believer as a promise
of the future work of the Spirit in us.

   This word for "guarantee" is used in only two other
places in Scripture, both times with the same reference:
the Spirit. The first verse is also in 2 Corinthians. In
1:22, Paul says "he has put his seal upon us and given
us his Spirit in our hearts as a guarantee." Nothing in
this passage specifically points to the Resurrection, but
in verse twenty-one one can see a hint of it in Paul's
describing our union with Christ: "it is God who es-
tablishes us with you in Christ." If we are established
with Christ and the Spirit is our guarantee of that, then
it is clear how our establishment with Christ is essential for us to be resurrected like He was (2 Cor. 5:4–5).

   The seal Paul mentions in 2 Corinthians 1:22 draws
us to the other passages where "guarantee" is used, such
as Ephesians 1:13–14. It is there that Paul says we "were
sealed with the promised Holy Spirit, which is the guarantee of our inheritance until we acquire possession of
it." Again, there is no clear reference to resurrection
here, but the reference in 2 Corinthians 5 leads us to
the conclusion that Paul is referring to our resurrec-

tion as, at least, an aspect of "our inheritance."
Furthermore, in Ephesians 4:30, Paul says we were sealed
with the Holy Spirit "for the day of redemption." This
seal for the "day of redemption" also helps to draw one's
mind to how we wait for "the redemption of our bodies." In fact, there is nothing in any of these passages
(2 Cor. 1:22, 5:5, Eph. 1:13–14, 4:30) which has a "near"
or "soon" focus forcing us to accept an A.D. 70 fulfillment; each passage is left open in regard to the time of
its fulfillment—this is clearly because Paul did not know
the day it would happen.

We have thus come full circle. The Spirit is residing
in us to give us a guarantee of our future resurrection,
and it is because of His presence that we "groan inwardly" in our desire to see the "redemption of our
bodies." We groan because our redeemed spirits want a
redeemed body to live in (see also 2 Cor. 5:1–4). The
distinction Paul is making with "adoption" in verses fifteen and twenty-three is evident from his usage. In verse
fifteen , he refers to a "spirit of adoption" (or "adopted
spirit") we have already received, and says in verse sixteen that it is our spirit which is affected by this; it is
an adoption of our spirit. In verse twenty-three, however, Paul says we have not yet received adoption and
that we are waiting for it. What makes this "adoption"
different is that he equates our "adoption" with the "redemption of our bodies." We have already received adoption as sons in our spirit; we have not yet received adoption
as sons in our bodies.

Some pantelists have tried to say that Paul is here
speaking of the redemption of the "body" of the Church
as the "body of Christ" because Paul uses the singular
"body" in verse twenty-three. The reason he uses a singular form there is plain: he is referring to each and
every Christian body as in 1 Corinthians 6:19, where
he says "your (plural) body (singular) is a temple of
the Holy Spirit." There he is not referring to the Church

as the body of Christ as the context (6:12–20) shows. Paul is not saying they cannot unite the Church as a whole with a prostitute, but that they cannot unite their individual bodies with a prostitute. He makes the clearest distinction possible in verse 15 of this same chapter when he says "your bodies are members of Christ," thus showing that the individual physical bodies of believers make up the entire "body of Christ," which is the Church.

An additional point can be made from Romans 6:12, where we find Paul speaking about "your mortal body" in the singular because he is referring to their individual bodies not being given over to sin because they have been spiritually brought "from death to life" already. Therefore in Romans 8:23, Paul says "our (plural) body (singular)" because he wants to show that each and every believer's body in the true Church of Christ will be redeemed. Furthermore, in verses ten and eleven, Paul clearly refers to "your bodies" in the plural. One last point should cement this idea: nowhere in Scripture is the Church as the body of Christ ever referred to as "our body" or "your body" but always as "His body" (e.g., Rom. 12:5; 1 Cor. 10:17; 12:12ff; Eph. 1:23; 5:30). The Church is not "our body." If we begin to think so, we have some serious problems with understanding that we in the Church represent Christ; we do not represent ourselves. The burden of proof is clearly on the pantelist to show Paul is here speaking of anything other than the physical resurrection of our fallen physical bodies.

*8:24—For in this hope we were saved. Now hope that is seen is not hope. For who hopes for what he sees?* The concept of "hope" and its relation to the resurrection cannot be examined in full here. We will, however, see the importance of Paul's usage of hope within this context. Hope is noticeably central to this passage. Paul says creation was subjected "in hope" (8:20) of being set free. He also says we were (past tense) saved in hope (thus, hope of something future). What is it that Paul is hoping for? Whatever our interpretation of verse twenty-three, Paul is saying he was saved in hope of "the redemption of our bodies." That is the immediate antecedent to the word "hope," and this connects best with the "hope" that creation was subjected in (i.e., hope of its redemption).

Crucial to this passage is another passage that is found in 1 Corinthians. Paul says in 1 Corinthians 13:13: "So faith, hope, love abide, these three; but the greatest of these is love." Why is love the greatest? Because it is eternal. Love is not centered in what is not seen like faith and hope are. Hope, as we have seen, is centered on what is not seen (Rom. 8:24). Faith is likewise centered on the unseen (Heb. 11:1). Therefore when the "unseen" becomes "seen," faith and hope are no longer necessary. We will not need to have faith in God in eternity. He will be right there before us, and we will know firsthand all that He says. Paul describes our time "away from the Lord" (2 Cor. 5:6) as walking by "faith, not by sight" (2 Cor. 5:7). He is saying that once we are "at home with the Lord" (2 Cor. 5:8), we will not walk by faith but by sight because we will see him face to face. Neither will we need to have hope in what God will do because He will have done it. Love, however, "never ends" (1 Cor. 13:8), because we will love not only each other but, most especially, God for all eternity.[15] Faith and hope disappearing someday should not surprise us; though the Word of God remains forever, the Scriptures will not be necessary for us in eternity.

*8:25—But if we hope for what we do not see, we wait for it with patience.* Here Paul is finishing what he said in the previous verse. He says we wait "with patience" because we do not see it. If we were able to see it we would not be able to have patience (this principle is the reason behind the hiding of a child's birthday gifts until it's time to open them). If, however, the pantelist is right and this is a spiritual thing Paul is speaking of, then we would never "see" it;[16] we would only "experience" it. You see something that is physical, like a physical resurrection body.

From this exegesis we can see that Paul is discussing here in Romans 8 the renewal of the physical creation that was "subjected to futility" and put in "bondage to decay" by God at the fall of man. The connections made in this passage between the renewal of the physical earth and the resurrection of our physical body is too strong to be missed. As a result we should conclude that the physical creation awaits a day in which it will be regenerated (returned to the life it had before the fall of man) and thus delivered from death (its present experience of decay). Paul is certainly not specific on what that new world will be like, but we can gather that it will be like a new "Eden," only better. He also leaves open the timing for this event; the one time Paul uses a word that could have a "near" reference (8:18, "is to be" vs. "about to be"), the primary meaning of the word ("will certainly take place"[17]) fits the context better. Paul himself clearly had no idea when or how it was to take place. He only knew that it would. Needless speculation about the details will only get us into dangerous ground. As with the Final Advent, the details are left vague. We are only told that it is to happen. We can confidently realize that our "groaning" desire for redemption and for the world's release from "bondage to decay" will someday be a reality. It is not wishful thinking.

*Notes:*

[1] If the cross was, theologically, the central event of all history, there is nothing to say that God could not also make it the central event chronologically. This would imply that since the earth is (at the most) ten thousand years old (by biblical reckoning, not scientific myths), there would have been about eight thousand years before the cross and two thousand since the cross. Hence we could expect another six thousand years before Christ returns. This is not something that can be either proved or disproved by the Scriptures but is merely a matter of opinion based on Scriptural patterns. But it goes to show that there are redemptive-historical reasons to reject "doom and gloom." Another thought is that if God started showing steadfast love to a "thousand generations" of those who loved Him in 1400 B.C., then (with a generation being about forty years) that would mean that today we have another 36,600 years of history.

[2] The error of the "old-earthers," which says death and disease existed before the fall of man for millions of years, will not even be a consideration here—its falsity is self-evident.

[3] In fact, if "suffering" is necessary for a Christian to be glorified with Christ (8:17), then it cannot refer to the specific suffering under the Jews of the first century or under Nero in his persecution. If it did refer to those sufferings exclusively, then the vast majority of Christians (including every one of them alive today) would be excluded from glory. This must refer to suffering for Christ in general by every Christian, and thus the "present time" still refers to our day and not merely pre–A.D. 70.

[4] Notice the close proximity of 2 Corinthians 5:17 to 2 Corinthians 4:14–5:10. Although Paul looks forward to a future "new creation" of "glory" (2 Cor. 4:17; 5:1), he sees no contradiction in pointing out that there is a "new creation" that had already come for him. The pantelist may want to point to 2 Corinthians 5:17 to show that the new creation came in A.D. 70, but Paul wrote this almost twenty years before Jerusalem was destroyed.

[5] ὑπετάγη, aor. pass. With no clear subject named, Paul is obviously using a divine passive and cannot therefore be referring to the fall of the spiritual "heavens and earth." It was Adam who brought corruption to his own spiritual dominion, not God. God brought "futility" to the physical earth.

[6] τῆς δουλείας τῆς φθορᾶς

[7] ἀφθαρσία and ἄφθαρτός

[8] ἀθανασία, which clearly refers to physical immortality.

[9] We, of course, acknowledge that Peter in 2 Peter 3 interprets Isaiah 65:17ff as the coming of a new order of "heaven and earth" in A.D. 70. If, however, Paul uses the idea of "new creation" in reference to a past event in 2 Corinthians, the pantelist is hard-pressed

to prove that Paul is changing his usage in Romans 8 to fit with 2 Peter 3 rather than remaining consistent with his own usage elsewhere. Because Peter chooses to use an image to describe A.D. 70 does not mean Paul (in an earlier letter) is pressed to abide by the same image (especially if he clearly considers the image in a different way in 2 Cor. 5).

[10] The assertion that we are "delivered from sin" is not an avowal of sinless perfection but rather an acknowledgment that sin "is not our master." It is, however, a denial that Paul is discussing the experience of a Christian in Romans 7:14f (see Ridderbos, Herman, *Paul.* [Grand Rapids, MI: Eerdmans Pub. Co. 1975] pp. 126–130). Though my conviction is firm on this issue, I acknowledge that there are great minds on both sides.

[11] ἀπαρχή, a Jewish technical term referring to something set apart to God before the rest was used. Here one can see it is the first dispensing of the Spirit for spiritual resurrection before He works in physical resurrection.

[12] τά θνητά σώματα, where θνητός and its relation to θνήσκω show its meaning to be "one subject to physical death." In addition σώματα is plural and thus refers to the physical bodies of individual believers.

[13] ἀρραβών, "first instalment (sic), deposit . . . pledge . . . a payment which obligates the contracting party to make further payments," *BAG*, p. 109.

[14] This "further clothed" in itself necessitates a physical resurrection. What else could the soul that loses the body ("the earthly tent we live in") be *further* clothed with, if not another physical body?

[15] If, however, the pantelist is right and the world goes on forever as it does now, then faith and hope will be eternal also. Love will not be the only thing that remains in eternity, because Christians will still need to live by faith and hope, forever and ever.

[16] Paul uses βλέπω, which almost always refers to physical sight. If he had used οἶδα, it would be possible to imagine that he was referring to a mental perception. βλέπω makes this a slim possibility.

[17] See *BAG*, p. 500.

# Chapter Four

# Judgment Day

THE CONCEPT OF JUDGMENT HAS BEEN REWORKED BY THE pantelists to the point of a full denial of the orthodox teaching of a future Day of Judgment at the end of this world. It is not enough to merely mention the verses in Scripture which refer to "judgment" or to a "Day of Judgment," for these have not been denied by the pantelists. Although they use various angles to deny a Final Judgment, they share this common thread: by the destruction of Jerusalem in A.D. 70, the references to a Judgment Day were fulfilled entirely. There is nothing left in the Scriptures that is future to us in any way. Pantelists will either say that talk of a judgment day refers only to the judgment that was brought upon Israel, or that it does refer to everyone who ever lived—it is just a spiritual judgment. This second option is often described as a secret event that took place outside the purview of the physical world.

## Jesus' Comparison
In sending out the twelve apostles, Jesus gave a special commission that limited their preaching. He told them, "If any one will not receive you or listen to your words, shake off the dust from your feet as you leave that house or town" (Matt. 10:14). This rejection that the hardhearted would give to the apostles was not, how-

ever, of the same caliber as previous instances where
people had rejected the word of God. For this time it
was not the promise of Christ's coming that they were
rejecting but Christ Himself. Our Lord uses one of the
most sinful groups of people in all the Scriptures to
show how bad it was for the Jews to reject Him. Affirming it with an oath—"Truly, I say to you, it shall be
more tolerable on the day of judgment for the land of
Sodom and Gomorrah than for that town" (Matt. 10:15).

The question we must ask is, What do the inhabit-
ants of a city that had been dead for two thousand years
have to do with the judgment on apostate Israel? This
question is most difficult to answer from a pantelist perspective. The "judgment" of A.D. 70 was obviously a
temporal judgment on the Jews who crucified Christ.
Although it had consequences that would affect all Christians for the rest of history, it is a stretch to try to
make any connection between Israel who killed Christ
and two towns of Gentile sexual perverts that were destroyed five hundred years before the nation of Israel
came into existence.

Now Sodom and Gomorrah are certainly a biblical
paradigm for evil,[1] but their sin was not an open rejection of God incarnate, as it was for Jesus' contemporary generation. They did not have the light that was
given to the Jews of the first century. Jesus specifically
says the judgment for Sodom and Gomorrah (i.e., in
the future and thus separate from the temporal punishment they experienced two millennia before) would not
be as bad as the judgment that would be meted out on
the Jews who rejected Christ. He refers to the judgment of Sodom and Gomorrah as being completely a
future event. This in itself causes numerous problems
for the pantelist. Jude says Sodom and Gomorrah underwent "a punishment of eternal fire" (Jude 7), referring to their *temporal* destruction two thousand years
before. Yet Jesus here says they will, on "judgment day,"

come into judgment again. The paradigm is obvious. Sodom and Gomorrah underwent a temporal judgment that did not exclude them from an eternal judgment at the end of all things.

Now we know the temporal judgment that was meted out on Israel in A.D. 70 was future, but Jesus portrays here a single event ("the day of judgment") that will bring not only apostate Israel to judgment but also Sodom and Gomorrah. J. Stuart Russell, a pantelist from the nineteenth century, tries to say that Jews of prior centuries will be brought to judgment in A.D. 70, but he acknowledges that pagans cannot be included as well.[2]

This is not, however, the only comparison our Lord makes with this idea. In other texts, He compares apostate Jews to other wicked groups by upbraiding the unrepentant within particular cities. In the same passage He condemns Chorazin, Bethsaida, and Capernaum. These first two cities Jesus compares to "Tyre and Sidon," and in a similar fashion, He says that it "should be more tolerable on the day of judgment for Tyre and Sidon than for those cities" (Matt. 11:22).

Let us consider Tyre and Sidon for a moment. They were Phoenician cities that were definitely outside of the Old Covenant. There are plenty of prophecies against Tyre found in the Old Testament (Ezek. 26:3–21; Amos 1:9; Joel 3:4–6), as well as against Sidon (Is. 23:12; Jer. 27:3–6; Ezek. 28:20–24; Joel 3:4–6). There is no doubt that once again our Lord is using these cities as a paradigm of evil, and thus he is showing that those who rejected Him are to become a new paradigm to replace the old ones.

It is most evident from the rest of Matthew that Jesus is not talking here about the contemporary generation of those in Tyre and Sidon (and thus it cannot somehow be included within the experience of the Jewish war). The reason for this is that the testimony we have of Jesus' experience in Tyre and Sidon is in accord with the rest of the testimony of Gentile acceptance (e.g., Matt. 8:11–12). In Matthew 15 (and its parallels), we find the one recorded instance of Jesus visiting the region of Tyre and Sidon. I will not go through the entire passage. I will merely mention Jesus' words that give us testimony about the people of that region: "Great is your faith!" (Matt. 15:28). The example of the present Tyre and Sidon is that they have "great faith" while the Jews are faithless. These people did not have anything to "tolerate" on the Day of Judgment. Rather it was the Tyre and Sidon that had been condemned in the past, and thus they had no experience of the Lord incarnate or of the Jewish war in the first century. This is exactly the same pattern found with Sodom and Gomorrah.

The same questions must be asked here as before: What do two Gentile towns outside of the realm of the people of God have to do with the judgment that would come upon Jerusalem in A.D. 70? The answer is again clear: nothing. They do, however, have everything to do with a final Judgment Day that will be experienced by everyone who ever lived. Jesus has no theological or practical reason to include Sodom and Gomorrah in His reference to the temporal judgment that was experienced by Jerusalem in 70. He does, however, have reason to include them in a reference to the Last Judgment at the end of the world.

One final passage carries this note in it, and it uses two different points of comparison than previously. After calling the contemporary generation "evil and adulterous" (Matt. 12:39), Jesus says the men of Ninevah will "arise at the judgment with this generation and condemn it" (12:41). He gives a clear reference to the ancient nature of the people He is referring to by pointing to their repentance under the preaching of Jonah (12:41). Christ does not here mention the issue of "more tolerable" judgment than Israel's because He is discussing the Ninevites. Again, what does Ninevah (specifically a particular generation of Ninevites who died out eight hundred years before Christ) have to do with the destruction of Jerusalem in the first century? In the pantelist scheme of things, nothing. In an orthodox understanding of Judgment Day at the end of all things, Ninevah has much to do with Israel's judgment. The other comparison we have to look at is the next verse in the previous context. Jesus there says that the "queen of the South" will also arise at the judgment to condemn the contemporary generation of Jews. What has been said above about Ninevah also rings true here. The "queen of the South" (or queen of Sheba) lived a thousand years before Christ. She also can be seen to have been open to the word of the Lord by her listening to the "wisdom of Solomon" (12:42). She too will condemn Israel on the last day.

There is also a most interesting factor to be included at this point from this last passage. Both the Ninevites and the queen of the South are said to "arise" in the judgment to condemn the Jews.[3] One can then assume that if this judgment Jesus speaks of is occurring in A.D. 70, we would need to resurrect the Ninevites and the queen of the South, who were long dead. But that is not all that Jesus says. He says they will arise "with this generation" (12:41, 42).[4] Jesus is saying that "this generation" will "arise" (be physically resurrected) at the judgment just as much as the centuries-dead queen of the South and the men of Ninevah.

Let me explain this point in more depth. The assumption by our Lord that "this generation" would need to be resurrected physically in order to stand at the judgment is in complete contrast with the passages that speak of the judgment the Jews of the first century would experience in their lifetime. Jesus told His apostles (who were the faithful part of "this generation") that some of them would live to see His "coming" (Matt.16:28, notice the "judgment" aspect of the previous verse).

He said Israel would be judged *before* "this generation" was to "pass away" (i.e., before they were to die) (Matt. 24:34). He said the high priest would see (i.e., in his lifetime) Christ seated at the "right hand of Power" (Matt. 26:64). This leads us to the conclusion that the entire contemporary generation was not in need of resurrection because there were enough alive when Jesus came against Jerusalem to fulfill this prophecy (this is one of the basic points that makes one believe Jesus came in judgment in the first century).

If Jesus were speaking of a Day of Judgment which would require "this generation" (not merely a few, but all of them in "this generation") to be resurrected, then He must have been speaking about something that was far enough away in time for all of "this generation" to have died, and thus after A.D. 70. In addition, Christ was speaking of something that included people from other eras who have no connection at all with the rejection of Christ in the first century A.D. For it was that generation, and that one alone, that was to be punished for killing Christ (Matt. 23:32–36), not people who lived in Sodom two thousand years before.

### Exclusively "This Generation"

In connection with these passages, pantelists have proposed that the "judgment" of A.D. 70 included not only apostate Jews but also (in some way) every person alive at the time (even Gentiles living thousands of miles away). Some (as noted above) have even said the "judgment" included all those who were within the nation of Israel from previous generations as well. They do this because they are sincerely trying to interpret the Scriptures faithfully. The Bible gives us "universal" statements about the Last Judgment like the following:

> He has fixed the day on which he will judge the world in righteousness by a man whom he has appointed, and of this

he has given assurance to all men by raising him from the dead. (Acts 17:31)

For we shall all stand before the judgment seat of God; for as it is written, "As I live, says the Lord, every knee shall bow to me, and every tongue shall give praise to God." So each of us shall give account of himself to God. (Rom. 14:10–11)

For we must all appear before the judgment seat of Christ, so that each one may receive good or evil, according to what he has done in the body. (2 Cor. 5:10)

The threat of judgment upon numbers of people who don't live in Jerusalem, as well as to people who did not specifically reject Christ, forces pantelists to say the temporal judgment on apostate Israel in the first century included everyone alive at the time. This, however, does not harmonize with the references to the judgment on Israel in A.D. 70. Look at a few references which describe the nature, cause, and purpose of the judgment Christ brought upon Jerusalem in 70:

You brood of vipers! Who warned you to flee from the wrath to come? Bear fruit that befits repentance. . . . Even now the axe is laid to the root of the trees; every tree that does not bear good fruit is cut down and thrown into the fire. (Matt. 3:7–10)

An evil and adulterous generation seeks for a sign, but no sign shall be given to it except the sign of Jonah. (Matt. 16:4)

O faithless and perverse generation, how long am I to be with you? (Matt. 17:17)

Whoever is ashamed of me and of my words in this adulterous and sinful generation, of him will the Son of man also be ashamed, when he comes in the glory of his Father with the holy angels. (Mark 8:38)

> These are days of vengeance to fulfill all that is written.
> ... For great distress shall be upon the earth and wrath upon
> this people... for it will come upon all who dwell upon the
> face of the whole [land (of Palestine)]. (Luke 21:22–23, 35)

> Men of Israel ... this Jesus, delivered up according to the
> definite plan and foreknowledge of God, you crucified and
> killed by the hands of lawless men. (Acts 2:22–23)

> And he testified with many other words and exhorted them
> saying, "Save yourselves from this crooked generation."
> (Acts 2:40)

From these verses we can see that the focus of the condemnation in the first century was upon the Jews who
rejected Christ. So often does this condemnation occur that the idea of "this generation" becomes a technical term to describe the apostate Jews who refused to
accept Jesus as the Messiah (see also Acts 7:51–53;
13:32–47; 1 Thess. 2:14–16). This is all an echo of the
warning given in Deuteronomy 18:15–19. There Moses
prophesied the coming of the "prophet" like Moses (who
was Christ) and warned that they should not reject Him
when He comes (see also Acts 3:22f).

The issue of the judgment on Israel was not sin in
general but most specifically the sin of rejecting the
Messiah. The special judgment in A.D. 70 is not directed
at the Roman empire per se, nor to any Gentile in particular; it is a punishment particularly on "this generation" who rejected Christ.

The references to universal judgment make no sense
in the context of a punishment on the apostate Jews of
the first century. Titus was not a Jew, he did not reject
Christ, and he did not live in Palestine (i.e., he was not
included in "this generation"), yet Paul told him to live
a godly life so that when Jesus comes he will be prepared (Titus 2:11–14). Timothy was only half Jewish,
did not live in Palestine, and did not reject Christ, yet

Paul commanded him to "keep the commandment un-
stained and free from reproach until the appearing of
our Lord Jesus Christ" (1 Tim. 6:14). How do these
warnings of judgment fit with the coming of Christ in
70 against Jerusalem?

The uncontested passages (which clearly refer to
the destruction of Jerusalem in 70) all bear clear reference to the nature of that judgment: it is centered in
Palestine ("the whole land" Luke 21:35) and involved
the Jews who rejected Christ ("ashamed of me . . . in
this adulterous and sinful generation" Mark 8:38). The
only note of effect this event has upon anyone else is,
first, in the Neronic persecution resulting from man-
datory emperor worship (and the clearest descriptions
of this occur in the book of Revelation), and second, in
the blessings that will come for the Church once she is
delivered from her persecutors. The only judgment and
condemnation given are against the apostate Jews (for
their rejection of Christ and their persecution of the
Church) and perhaps Rome (for demanding emperor
worship). Furthermore, the notes of punishment on
Rome, which are confined to the book of Revelation
(14:9–11; 16:10; 17:8, 11, 14; 19:19–20), are few and
focused on Nero. Rome is more often viewed positively
than negatively in the New Testament. Before the
Neronic persecution, Rome protected the Church. During the Jewish war, Rome was the "servant of God" against
Israel (as Babylon was in Jer. 25:8–9). In the person of
Nero we find the first antagonism between Rome and
the Church.

The manner in which Christ "destroyed" Rome is
not the same as that in which He destroyed Israel. Israel received physical destruction and punishment at
the hands of Rome. Rome was "punished" by having
her gods destroyed when the majority of the empire
was converted. It was a long and slow process before
Rome fell in any physical fashion (over three hundred

years later). Christ "destroyed" Rome by "the sword
that issues from his mouth" (Rev. 19:21), which is the
word of God (i.e., He converted them rather than killing them). Nero is clearly portrayed as having a brutal
death (see Rev. 13:10 as a reference to Nero's death by
sword, and 19:20 as a reference to the torture he went
through: "thrown alive"). The image given of the Romans, other than Nero, is much more peaceful. Taking
the "sharp sword" that comes from Christ's mouth, in
Revelation 19:15, as the gospel, it is clear "the rest" of
the Roman empire was "slain by the sword of him who
sits upon the horse" (Rev. 19:21). They were converted
by the gospel of Jesus Christ Almighty. This was indeed more of a blessing than a punishment.

We see from two pivotal texts that the cause for the
coming of Christ in 70 was Jewish apostasy, and the
purpose was the destruction of those very same apos-
tates:

> Therefore I send you prophets and wise men and scribes,
> some of whom you will kill and crucify, and some you will
> scourge in your synagogues and persecute from town to
> town, that upon you may come all the righteous bloodshed
> on earth. . . . Truly, I say to you, all this will come upon this
> generation. (Matt. 23:34–36)

> Therefore also the wisdom of God said, "I will send them
> prophets and apostles, some of whom they will kill and
> persecute" that the blood of all the prophets, shed from the
> foundation of the world, may be required of this generation.
> . . . Yes, I tell you, it shall be required of this generation.
> (Luke 11:49–51)

These two instances, where Jesus gives the same truth,
clearly state the core of the judgment in 70 is to be on
the generation of Jews that crucified Christ. To try to
force the descriptions of Judgment Day, which have a
universal note to them, into the events of the Jewish

war and the Roman persecution of the Church is like putting a square peg in a round hole.

This is where the pantelist not only is heterodox but also ends up contradicting his pantelism itself. In order to maintain that Christ did "come" in judgment in A.D 70, they rightly interpret and emphasize the contemporary nature of the prophecies. Nevertheless, when they examine the prophecies about the Last Judgment, they have to ignore the contemporary nature of the other passages in order to fit the universal Judgment within the frame of the temporal judgment on Israel. These two ideas don't fit, and they need to compromise the truth of preterism in order to remain pantelists. Many prophecies in the New Testament have already been fulfilled; that is why we say they are past. Some, however, have not been fulfilled; they clearly display a coming of Christ, a Judgment, and a Resurrection that include everyone who ever lived and bring an end to this physical world.

This is where we see the pantelist acting like a dispensationalist. The dispensationalist de-emphasizes the contemporary nature of the prophecies about A.D. 70 in order to make them fit with the Final Advent. The pantelist de-emphasizes the contemporary nature of the prophecies about A.D. 70 in order to make the prophecies of the Final Advent fit with them. Both are wrong.

### The Living and the Dead
In the book of Romans, Paul often speaks to the issues that could easily divide the Jews and Gentiles in the Roman church. In chapter fourteen Paul gives an exhortation for those who had differences to bear with one another and ends with this comment:

> If we live, we live to the Lord, and if we die, we die to the Lord; so then whether we live or whether we die, we are the Lord's.

For to this end Christ died and lived again, that he might be Lord both of the dead and of the living. Why do you pass judgment on your brother? Or you, why do you despise your brother? For we shall all stand before the judgment seat of God; for it is written, "As I live, says the Lord, every knee shall bow to me, and every tongue shall give praise to God." So each of us shall give account of himself to God. (Rom. 14:8–12)

The issues Paul pleads with the Roman church to bear with are things Christians can acceptably disagree over. He thus urges their compliance because these are not things that must be resolved on this side of "the judgment seat of God."

In verses eight and nine, Paul is speaking about Christians; whether alive or dead they belong to Christ. Once a Christian dies, he does not suddenly become released from his submission to Christ as Lord. David was only able to be king over those who were alive, and only while he himself was alive. Christ, however, reigns over all believers whether alive or dead.[5] Since He reigns over them even in death, it would be wrong for the Roman Christians to insist that all things are "judged" (14:10) now in this life. God will ensure that everyone gives account of himself. The giving of account must be an event that occurs after death for every believer. He is saying that for every believer there will be an accounting before God after he has died.

The point of contention should be obvious: is Paul speaking of a Final Judgment or not? The pantelist, who denies any kind of Final Judgment, has only two options for interpreting this passage. First, he can say all who were either alive or dead at the coming of Christ in A.D. 70 were eternally judged (which would leave millions of Christians and non-Christians that had not yet been born free from eternal judgment). Second, he can say that after each person dies he faces Christ in judgment (which would leave the reference to the "living" being judged pointless).

### Peter and Cornelius

We can find help interpreting this passage from other passages which speak similarly. The phrase "living and dead" is used with a similar context in three other passages in the New Testament, and each time, the author connects the phrase with the "judgment" of Christ.

In Acts 10, Peter tells Cornelius that after Jesus died, was resurrected, and was witnessed as alive by those God had chosen, "he commanded us to preach to the people, and to testify that he is the one ordained by God to be judge of the living and the dead" (10:42). In this instance we find that Peter recognizes that God has reached out to Cornelius, a Gentile, and brought salvation to him. Peter is therefore not dealing with an unrepentant group of Jews who killed Christ and were rejecting His apostles (as in Acts 3:11–26). As a result, he is not concerned so much with the punishment on Jerusalem that was going to come. He did not have to warn Cornelius to save himself "from this crooked generation" (Acts 2:40). God sent Cornelius to Peter, not the other way around!

Accordingly, we have no reason to infer that Peter was warning Cornelius of the judgment coming on Jerusalem. There are no references to "nearness" in this passage; none of the available terms used to denote an imminent fulfillment of this judgment are found here. In fact the usage has a very universal note to it: "judge of the living and the dead," whoever they may be, whenever they may live and die. Consequently, this passage tends more towards Christ's sovereignty and authority over all things than specifically to any act of judgment (though this is not excluded in the context). The preaching of the apostles most often included a reference to Christ's exaltation (e.g., Acts 2:32f; 4:10f; 5:30f). In Peter's preaching to Cornelius, the reference to "judge of the living and dead" is Peter's way of saying that Christ has been exalted to the highest place possible, the judge of everyone who ever lived.

### Paul's Death

The next usage of "living and dead" occurs in the last letter of Paul. In 2 Timothy, he says to Timothy, "I charge you in the presence of God and of Christ Jesus who is to judge the living and the dead, and by his appearing and his kingdom" (4:1). Paul here makes reference to Jesus as the One who is to "judge the living and the dead" and connects that event with "his appearing, and his kingdom." The difficulty with this passage is that Paul is here using terminology that has also been used to refer to the destruction of Jerusalem. We will see, however, that Jerusalem's destruction does not fit in this context.[6]

Paul is exhorting Timothy to be strong because he knows that he is going to die soon: "the time of my departure has come" (4:6). He thus wants Timothy to continue to serve God as Paul had for years. It is this service and perseverance that gives Paul confidence about appearing before God. He says in verse eight: "Henceforth there is laid up for me the crown of righteousness, which the Lord, the righteous judge, will award to me on that Day, and not only to me but also to all who have loved his appearing." Paul's usage of "righteous judge" and "his appearing" makes an obvious connection to what he mentioned in verse one. Thus verse eight helps us to understand Paul's mind in verse one. Although the pantelist assumes 4:1 is referring to events in the first century, this is not necessitated by anything in the text. This becomes apparent when one realizes that Paul viewed the Final Advent of Christ as an event which all believers will be present for (as in 1 Cor. 15:23; 1 Thess. 4:15–17; etc.). This is also the view we see presented in verse eight: "not only to me but also to all who have loved his appearing." The event Paul is speaking of in 2 Timothy 4:1–8 somehow involves all Christians. The destruction of Jerusalem may have had repercussions for Christians of all time, but it cannot be said that all Christians were involved in what happened in A.D. 70.

Once again, Paul is speaking here about an event that takes place after his death, in which he received a reward from Christ for his faithfulness. He also sees this event as including all Christians who ever lived. Even if we allow for a moment that Paul is referring to A.D. 70, we have problems. Christians who are alive today look back and love the "appearing" of Christ that took place at the destruction of Jerusalem. Does that mean we somehow received a "crown of righteousness" before we were ever faithful? How could we have received a crown when we had not yet been born and not yet come to Christ? The crown is the reward of a faithful life—how could it come before that life?

What we have here is an event that happens after Paul's death, where all Christians are rewarded for their faithfulness. Why does Paul see it as coming after his death? How did he know Jesus would not come before his death and reward him then? Paul not only knew that Christ's coming against Jerusalem was near, he also knew he could not know the exact day of that event. If he were speaking about A.D. 70, it was possible he could have lived to see it. Paul knew the event of reward he was speaking of was so far in the future that he would be dead, as well as all the Christians of his day.

Paul calls Jesus the "righteous judge" and the "judge of the living and dead" in the same way that we saw Peter using the concept in Acts 10. Jesus is the divine sovereign over all and thus is the One who will judge everyone who has ever lived. Whether it is those who are living at His appearing or those who have already died, He is the judge of all (this same concept is seen in many places in the Scriptures; e.g., 1 Thess. 4:15ff.).

### Peter and the Gentiles

The last passage where "living and dead" is used in this fashion is found in 1 Peter. We read there: "[T]hey will give account to him who is ready to judge the living and the dead" (4:5). The context of the passage is that the "Gentiles" are trying to get the Christians to return to the sins they had participated in (4:3–4). Peter gives his readers confidence to endure by saying that the Gentiles who are tempting them will give account to Christ when He judges the "living and the dead." We find here an extension of the idea Paul was expressing in 2 Timothy. Paul said all Christians would receive reward at the judging of the "living and the dead." Here Peter says that Gentiles living in "Pontus, Galatia, Cappadocia, Asia, and Bithynia" (1 Pet. 1:1) will give account for tempting Christians to sin, and this at the same event.

In what sense can we imagine Gentiles in Asia Minor of the first century giving account for their deeds before Christ when He destroyed Jerusalem? If this event did happen in the first century, then the "judging" that Christ supposedly did upon them had little effect, for they continued to live on this earth and tempt Christians. If it is proposed by the pantelist that his eternal destiny was set at A.D. 70 and that it only had effect later when he actually died, then we must ask: Did the Church suddenly stop growing after 70? It must have if the eternal destiny of every unbeliever was set in 70. It would be years before anyone (at least in Asia Minor) could be converted, since they were at that time "judged." The exact opposite is true: the Church flourished after A.D. 70.

It becomes obvious that Peter here is speaking of the Final Judgment of all men at the end of all things in the future. Thus Peter's usage of "living and dead" fits

exactly with Paul's and the reference we found from
Peter earlier in Acts. Jesus will, at some unknown day
in the future, end the course of this earth and at that
time judge everyone who is alive ("the living") and
everyone who has died prior to that day ("the dead").
This is the point of Peter's encouragement to his readers. Whether the "Gentiles" that are tempting them are
alive or not, they will give account to Christ and will
thus be judged by Him; none can escape because they
did not receive punishment in this life.

The concept that all judgment occurs in this life is
the very point that Peter is trying to defeat (while it is
what many pantelists are trying to defend). This can
also be seen in the next few verses. Peter says,

> For this is the reason the gospel was preached even to those
> who are now dead, so that they might be judged according
> to men in regard to the body, but live according to God in
> regard to the spirit. The end of all things is near. Therefore
> be clear minded and self-controlled so that you can pray.
> (1 Pet. 4:6–7 NIV)

Why, I ask, does Peter consider verse six to be part of
the foundation of verse five ("for this is the reason")?
If verse five is speaking of anything other than the Final Judgment then verse six has no connection to verse
five. Peter says that though there are those who have
already died (and thus been "judged in the flesh like
men" because they appear to have died like everyone
else), they will not be left out of the judgment of the
"living and the dead." Whether a person is alive or dead,
a believer or an unbeliever, he will give account to God
and be judged by Him.

The concept that judgment occurs only in this life
and not in the next is what draws Peter's mind to the
topic of "the end of all things." Clearly his reference
to the "end" being "near" shows that he is referring in
this context to the end of all things in the Jewish age.

Peter tells his readers it is true that God does bring judgment on the living here and now and because it was coming soon they need to live holy lives. This, however, does not negate the judgment that will occur for all men (at the *ultimate* end of *all* things). It would be easy for his readers to think that if someone dies before the temporal judgment of A.D. 70 they would not be punished, but Peter reminds them there is a judgment that is eternal and that everyone, either living or dead, will appear there.

What, therefore, can we draw from this? It becomes quite clear that Paul in Romans 14 is speaking of an event in which every Christian who ever lived (as well as every unbeliever who ever lived) will "give account of himself" (14:12) to Christ at the "judgment seat of God" (14:10). Though various attempts have been made to make it appear that Paul is here speaking of the "judgment" that occurs at the point of a believer's conversion, this goes entirely against the purpose of the passage. Paul points out that Christ is Lord of the living and dead, and both will be judged by Him. "Living and dead" are clearly connected with what Paul said in 14:8 about living and dead Christians; he is not here writing about spiritual life and death. In addition, if he were referring to the believer's conversion, then that event would be in the past. Paul says "we *shall*" all be judged, not "we were judged."

### Things Done in the Body

In 2 Corinthians 5:10 we have one last passage that connects to Romans 14. Although we do not find the terms "the living and the dead," the concept cannot be missed in Paul's language. He blatantly points to the Christian experience before and after death. The context reads as follows:

> So we are always of good courage; we know that while we are at home in the body we are away from the Lord, for we

> walk by faith, not by sight. We are of good courage, and we
> would rather be away from the body and at home with the
> Lord. So whether we are at home or away, we make it our
> aim to please him. For we must all appear before the
> judgment seat of Christ, so that each one may receive good
> and evil, according to what he has done in the body.
> (2 Cor. 5:6–10)

Paul's usage of "in the body" and "away from the body"
is evidently related to his usage back in Romans of
"whether we live or whether we die, we are the Lord's"
(14:8). Paul is saying in 2 Corinthians that we seek to
please Christ (5:9) while "in the body" (5:10), because
we will be judged for what we have done in the body.
Paul is patently clear; the things done in the body will
someday be judged by Christ Almighty, after we have
left "this body." Paul's statement that the things that
were "done in the body" (past tense) will necessarily
be judged (in the future, after the deeds have been done)
allows for no other option. Unless we are freed from
having our deeds examined and receiving "good or bad,
according to what" we have done, then we too must be
awaiting a time when we will "appear before the judgment seat of Christ."

It would be a pitiful depreciation of justice were
we to say that all punishment and rewards occur in this
life. Yes, our actions have consequences that bring blessings and curses in this life, but we know all too well
that those who are righteous often suffer for their righteousness while the wicked get away with their deeds.
Were we to assume that the eternal justice of God is
finished on this earth without a final day of reckoning,
we would be no better than the atheists.

## Confidence in Judgment
In 1 John 4:17, we find the statement: "In this is love
perfected with us, that we may have confidence for the
day of judgment, because as he is so are we in this world."

John is saying here that divine love works in believers in such a way that we are given full confidence on the Day of Judgment. The next verse helps us to see that the confidence is in regard to not being punished: "For fear has to do with punishment, and he who fears is not perfected in love" (4:18).

Throughout this letter John is giving his readers the specific details of what it means to be a Christian, and by consequence he is also showing them what a falsely professing Christian looks and acts like. Love, both for God and for our Christian brothers, is essential to the Christian life. John says not only that "God is love" (4:16), but also that if someone says he is a believer but does not love, then he is not a true Christian (4:20–21). Thus we can see why John puts love forward as giving one "confidence for the day of judgment."

The question we must ask at this point is: What is John referring to by the words "day of judgment" in this passage? John does not use the word for "judgment" (in any form) in 1 John other than at 4:17. He does, however, use it in his gospel in various contexts. What we must remember at this time is that definitions of words must fit in their context. We cannot limit the definition in such a way that its meaning contradicts the rest of Scripture.[7] I mention this because we find John using the word "judgment" in two different ways. "Judgment" cannot mean the same thing in the two instances we are about to examine, or else John would be contradicting himself. In the gospel of John, we hear Jesus telling us that "he who hears my word and believes . . . does not come into judgment" (5:24). John here affirms what we find in many other places in Scripture: believers cannot be condemned (Rom. 8:1, 34).[8]

John is not, however, using the word "judgment" in a standard way here. "Judgment," as noted above, can be either for good or bad; only its context points to whether it is a judgment of condemnation or a judgment of blessing. The judgment John is speaking of here cannot be seen by those who believe in Christ. This is why he doesn't speak of judgment in the same way Paul does. In 2 Corinthians 5:10 (see above), Paul says believers will see judgment, and it will result in either "good or evil" according to their deeds. John says believers cannot come into judgment in John 5:24, and yet he also uses "judgment" in 1 John 4:17 in the same way as Paul. John knows he is using "judgment" in this way and that is why he distinguishes the "resurrection" that occurs at the time of this "judgment" as a "resurrection of life" (for the righteous) and a "resurrection of judgment" (for the unrighteous) in John 5:29. Whereas Paul says all come into judgment and distinguishes it as "good or evil," John says all are resurrected and distinguishes it as "of life" and "of judgment."

Let us now return to 1 John 4:17. John unequivocally says that believers will appear at the "day of judgment." He is clearly not using judgment in the same sense that he uses it in John 5:24. In 1 John we are judged; in the Gospel of John we are not judged (see also John 3:18). No matter what the pantelists want these verses to say, we cannot equate the two entirely different usages of "judgment" found in these texts.[9] If John 5:24 says believers have already experienced all the "judgment" they will ever see at the cross, then 1 John 4:17 contradicts that.

There is a point John makes in 1 John that helps us understand what he is referring to. He uses the word "confidence" three other times in 1 John, and one of those is clearly related to what he says here in 4:17. The second and fourth time it appears (3:21 and 5:14) refer to "confidence" in prayer. On the other hand, the context for the first appearance of "confidence" in 1 John is directly related to what is said in 4:17. John says:

> And now, little children, abide in him, so that when he
> appears we may have confidence and not shrink from him
> in shame at his coming... we are God's children now; it does
> not yet appear what we shall be, but we know that when he
> appears we shall be like him, for we shall see him as he is. And
> every one who thus hopes in him purifies himself as he is
> pure. (1 Jn. 2:28–3:3)

A full explication of this verse will come later, but we
can see here how John uses it. John is, in this passage,
connecting the "coming" of Christ with our being made
"like him" (resurrection). For what John says, we can
see that he also believes that "judgment" will occur at
that same time (4:17). John is concerned that his readers be perfect in love (4:17) and also that they abide in
Christ (2:28) so they will be confident when Christ
comes to judge and make them like Him.

Let us make a clear distinction at this point. In 4:17
John says that "as he is so are we in this world." Thus
in some sense John viewed the believer as already like
Christ. This would certainly not be a physical likeness:
Christ is resurrected and can never die again; His physical
existence is eternal while we still die. He must be referring to a spiritual similarity we have with Christ. The
context says that the way we are "as he is," is found
in the love of God. We love others as God does (see
4:16, 19, 20). Therefore we are like Christ in holiness,
only by virtue of what He has done (4:19). If John and
the believers of the first century were like Christ in
this manner, what likeness was John looking forward
to that he did not yet know the manner of (3:2)? If
spiritual likeness already exists, then only a physical
likeness is left.

In A.D. 70 any concern for standing confidently before Christ was based on whether a person had faith in
Christ. Those who believed in Christ were delivered
from the destruction of Jerusalem (Rev. 7:3, 18:4). John's
concern here is a specific judgment on every deed of

believers such that they could be "ashamed" before
Christ. What shame did believers have in 70 when Jerusalem was destroyed? This is a judgment like the one Paul
spoke of in Romans 14:10 and 2 Corinthians 5:10. In
A.D. 70, the "judgment" was on the apostate nation of
Israel; at the end of all things there will be a judgment
on everyone who ever lived.

### Angels in Judgment

A particular pantelist commitment I wish to examine
under this topic is the allegation made by pantelists that
the judgment that took place in 70 (which we agree with
in principle but not to the degree that they propose)
included all of the angels. Whether stated verbally or
not, this must be included in their theology because
the prophecies of judgment in the New Testament refer to the angels being judged, and since the pantelists
wish to contend that all prophecy has been fulfilled,
this too must be included.

First I will examine the passages which discuss the
eternal judgment on the fallen angels. There is a reference in the gospels that points to the fact that the demons knew they were to be judged:

> And when he came to the other side, to the country of the
> Gadarenes, two demoniacs met him, coming out of the
> tombs, so fierce that no one could pass that way. And
> behold, they cried out, "What have you to do with us, O Son
> of God? Have you come here to torment us before the
> time?" (Matt. 8:28–29)

Not only is there clear reference to the demons' knowledge that they would be "tormented,"[10] but we can also
see here that they knew there was a specifically appointed
time for that event (they said Jesus was there "before
the time").[11] They also knew that the time for them to
be tortured had not yet come. If this was, however,
merely a spiritual judgment that would allow them to

continue their influence in the world (as it exists today), then how would they know that the time they
were in was "before the time?" The demons must have
been aware that the Day of Judgment they were afraid
of would bring about a radical change in their existence.

The question that must be asked at this time is: Did
the demons receive eternal judgment in A.D. 70? If so,
then why are they still able to do so much in this world?
We acknowledge that their influence is greatly limited
(see Rev. 20:2; Col. 2:15; etc.). But limited and eternally judged are not the same thing; there is a radical
difference between these two ideas (if we could ask the
demons, they would admit there is quite a difference!).

### The Abyss

The parallel passage in Luke contains another factor that
is especially revealing. In Luke 8, we find a description
of the same incident, but before we are told that the
demons asked to be sent into the swine, something
amazing is added to the story. It says, "They begged
him not to command them to depart into the abyss"
(Luke 8:31).

As has been said before, the demons sometimes know
theology better than we do. Here we find the demons
distinguishing between "the abyss" and being "tortured."
Their first fear was of being tortured, but they also did
not want to be cast into the abyss. At this point we
must examine further what "the abyss" is. Other than a
reference in Romans 10:7 (which does not help our
discussion here), the only usage of this idea in the New
Testament is in Revelation. There are four contexts in
Revelation in which we find "the abyss" spoken of (which
is translated in our text as "bottomless pit").

The first usage is in chapter nine, where we find
that the bottomless pit is filled with demonic "locusts"
(9:3f). A star (or angel) is given the key to release these
demons (9:1). The name of the leader of these demons

in English means "destroyer" (9:11), and he is described as "the angel of the bottomless pit." From this we can be safe in describing the abyss as a place where demons are temporarily imprisoned (temporarily, because these, at least, were "released" in the Jewish war of the first century).

The next usage is in chapter eleven. We find only one reference there and it is very brief. It reads, "When they have finished their testimony, the beast that ascends from the bottomless pit will make war upon them and conquer them and kill them" (11:7). The "beast" (most probably either Satan himself, or Satan "incarnated" in the Roman empire) is shown to have his origin in the abyss. Thus we find that the abyss is not a permanent prison; those within can be (and are) let out to wreak havoc.

Chapter seventeen has a similar reference. We are once again told that "the beast" "is to ascend from the bottomless pit and go to perdition" (17:8). Here we find a reaffirmation of what was said before; the abyss is a temporary place of punishment before the final punishment.

The last reference in Revelation is likewise supportive of this idea. In 20:1–3 we find that an angel locks Satan up in the abyss to limit his activity, and in 20:7 he is released from his "prison"[12] to attack God's people once again. The result of this attack is a swift casting into the "lake of fire," where he "will be tormented day and night forever and ever" (Rev. 20:10).[13] Interestingly, the description of eternal punishment includes "torment," which is exactly what we found the demons distinguishing in Luke 8:31 from merely being cast into the abyss.

What can we conclude from this? The fallen angels can be either "free" to roam the earth, or they can be limited in their influence by being cast into the abyss where they suffer temporarily. Both of these possibilities are, however, clearly contrasted with the eternal torment of the "lake of fire," which has an appointed time (in comparison to the general torment of the abyss that can come at any time to the demons). Therefore the demons know there is a specific time of torment for them all as well as the possibility that they can be put into the abyss for temporary punishment.

What other passages help us to examine the judgment on the fallen angels? There are not many. The next one I will look at is in Matthew 25:31ff. I will look only at the description we find of the judgment on the "devil and his angels" (Matt. 25:41). The punishment on the demons in this passage is not at the forefront, but we do find two references that will help us. In verse forty-one, the description of hell is given as: "the eternal fire prepared for the devil and his angels." The primary purpose of hell is for Satan and his minions; the secondary purpose is for those who were not "given to the Son."

This judgment is not merely a temporal experience however. It is described specifically as "eternal fire" (25:41) and subsequently as "eternal punishment" (25:46). Since this includes both lost men and angels, it is impossible to attempt to equate it with the "abyss" (nowhere is the abyss described as the abode of anyone other than the demons). The judgment experienced here is not something temporary; it is eternal. Thus if fallen angels have already experienced this, they would not still be influencing this world. Unless the pantelists desire to prove that there is no demonic influence on the world around us, they are forced to admit that the demons have not yet been cast into eternal hell. Demons don't experience judgment after they die, since they don't die. So when does this happen?

There are a few other passages that are helpful. In 2 Peter 2:4, we find a description of the demons awaiting Final Judgment: "God did not spare the angels when they sinned, but cast them into hell and committed them to pits of nether gloom to be kept until the judgment." The term translated as "hell" (by all major translations) is not the standard term for hell.[14] This term ("tartarus") is used to describe the place where the wicked dead are punished. Although this idea by itself could be equated with eternal punishment in hell, Peter does not allow us to do that. He specifically says they are "kept until the judgment." He clearly perceives a difference between eternal punishment and the temporary punishment he is here describing. From this we can see that Peter is using the term "tartarus" to describe what elsewhere is described by the term "abyss"—a temporary place of punishment until the final and eternal punishment in hell itself.

Jude 6 provides a parallel passage (probably borrowing from 2 Peter). In that context, we find the exact same point being made: "The angels that did not keep their own position but left their proper dwelling have been kept by him in eternal chains in the nether gloom until the judgment of the great day." Jude even refers here to their "eternal chains," which may sound like a permanent state, yet he too says they are awaiting "the judgment of the great day." Jude's "nether gloom" is clearly the same as the "abyss." So when will Satan and the other demons be sent to hell? According to pantelism they either already have been, or they never will be (depending on how they interpret eternal condemnation).

### Abyss vs. Judgment

Let us compare what we have seen with the report of Satan's experience found in the book of Revelation in order to see one of the most severe problems with the pantelist position. In Revelation 12, John has a vision of the "great red dragon" (12:3). This dragon, after failing to destroy the woman's "child," finds himself losing a "war" in heaven and being "thrown down to the earth"

(12:4–9). His defeat is also referred to as being connected with the fact that "there was no longer any place for them in heaven" (12:8). Satan lost his place in heaven at the cross, where he was defeated (Col. 2:15) and cast down (John 12:31).

This casting down cannot be equated with his being cast into the abyss, for two reasons. In 12:12 there is a warning given that Satan is coming to the earth "in great wrath," thus relating that he is going to bring persecution to the saints (12:17). Second, in 20:3, where he is cast into the abyss, his power is limited. The limiting of his power is told as an encouragement. The casting down to earth is told as a warning: these do not fit together as being the same event.

After he is cast down, it is said that "he knows that his time is short" (12:12). Time for what? According to the pantelist scheme, it is his time until the final judgment. I have already pointed out how being thrown down cannot be equated with being thrown into the abyss, so for the pantelist, Satan would have to have been bound in the abyss sometime after Christ's death and resurrection and before A.D. 70. This is, however, exegetically impossible. Even if we go ahead and equate 12:9 with 20:2, we find we have made a mockery of the "thousand years" of his binding in the abyss. Hence to make the time shorter than forty years is even less possible.

Satan knows his "time is short." Does a short time do justice to the idea of a "thousand years"? With all of the references to time lengths (three and a half years, ten days, etc.) in Revelation, it is impossible to make the symbolism of a thousand years equate with a "short time." If a thousand years does not denote a long duration of time, then it has lost all of its symbolism. One of the debates between premillennialism and postmillennialism is whether the "millennium" must be limited to a thousand years or whether it can denote a long period of time of unknown duration. No one except the pantelist is trying to make it be less than a thousand years. What is the purpose of saying a thousand years if John does not want to refer to a long period of time?

What event, then, could the short time be waiting until? The next significant event in the history of the Church would be the destruction of Israel in A.D. 70, at which time Satan was bound and cast into the abyss. Satan knew he only had a short time (forty years) to stop the Church from growing up. This is why he is said (after realizing he is cast down and only has a short time to work) to go "off to make war on . . . those who keep the commandments of God and bear testimony to Jesus" (12:17); he wants to destroy the New Covenant Church.

An unfortunate situation has occurred with the chapter division at this point. The last sentence of 12:17 should really be connected to chapter thirteen. It reads "And he stood on the sand of the sea;" that is, the dragon (Satan) stood on the shore. He stood there in order to call out the beast of chapter thirteen. 13:1 reads "And I saw a beast rising out of the sea with ten horns and seven heads" (the same description given to the dragon in 12:3). Satan stood there to call up the beast of the Roman empire so he could make "war on the saints" (12:17; 13:7). When does he do this? Certainly not while he is bound with chains in the abyss. Rather, he does it as a last-ditch effort because he knows he failed in his persecution of the Church by means of the apostate Jews (12:11), so now he will turn to the person of Nero Caesar for help (13:18). This is a last-ditch effort because he knows his "time is short" before he is "bound . . . for a thousand years" (20:2f) and can no longer "deceive the nations" (i.e., use them for his own ends).

The Scriptures are clear that Satan was cast out of heaven at the time of Christ's death/resurrection/ascension (John 12:31; Col. 2:14–15; Rev. 12:5–12). Therefore we ask, if he was cast out in A.D. 30 (and his time was then short) when was he bound for a thousand years? Surely he was not bound between 30 and 70! That was when he was making his greatest assault against the people of God. Furthermore, it is clear that he is bound between his being cast out of heaven and his final condemnation. Pantelism, in essence, has already sought to destroy the "long term" statements of Scripture at the expense of saving the "short term" statements (a task which is wholly unnecessary). Now they have tried to squeeze a thousand years into a period of forty years. Even the dispensationalists haven't gone this far.

In addition, we find that the time of the destruction of the "beast and false prophet" (19:20) is removed from the time when Satan is destroyed (20:10). This is not merely an argument from the order of the vision in Revelation. In 20:10, John says that "the devil . . . was thrown into the lake of fire and sulphur where the beast and the false prophet were."[15] John says the beast and false prophet had *already* received their punishment before Satan did (at least a thousand years before). However, if the pantelist is correct, then this final deception that Satan brings would have been by means of the beast and false prophet (i.e., in the first century). They are, however, nowhere mentioned in this text (20:7–10).

In fact, the description in 20:9 of the "final battle" is completely inadequate as a description of the Jewish war in 70. Immediately after the "camp of the saints and the beloved city" is surrounded, "fire . . . from heaven" destroys Satan and his armies. The Jewish war lasted three and a half years. This war appears to last a few minutes. Furthermore, in the Jewish war, Jerusalem is not the camp of "the saints." They abandoned Jerusalem and consigned it to the flames (Matt. 24:16; Rev. 18:4). And when the Jewish war ended, the "holy city" of Jerusalem was destroyed, and the Romans survived. Here in Revelation 20:9, the city is preserved and the armies are destroyed. This is the exact opposite of A.D. 70 at all points. Satan and (at least some, if not all of) his demons are presently limited in their efforts because they are chained in the abyss. They are awaiting the "judgment of the great day" which will occur a long time after they were first incarcerated in the abyss (not a mere forty years). They are still awaiting this now, in spite of what is claimed by the pantelists.[16]

Finally, we see that Judgment Day is described in Revelation as something that is in the distant future (at least a thousand years after A.D. 70). It does not carry the idea in any way that it is something which is "at hand." In fact, if we are consistent with the idea of prophecy being "near," we will realize that even the destruction of Jerusalem was not as "near" as the *beginning* of the war. The beginning of the Jewish war was "near," the end of the Jewish war was three and a half years away. In comparison with the nearness of a few months, three and a half years is quite a wait. What John's primary reference is pointing at is that the beginning of the three and a half years is "near." The end of the three and a half years is (of course) at least three and a half years away. With this in mind, we can see that the beginning of the thousand years was "near," the end of the thousand years was (at least) one thousand years away. Therefore, it is evident that John viewed the judgment found in 20:7–15 as being in the distant future. Once again, the judgment on the demons is still future. It will occur on the same day as the judgment of all men, the day that is clearly spoken of throughout Scripture: Judgment Day. Pantelism cannot scripturally answer this difficulty.

### "Nearness" and the Old Testament
Much of the problem with pantelism is the same problem that can be attributed not only to dispensationalism but also to every system that rejects the preterist fac-

tors of Scriptures. Nonpreterist systems either ignore
or reinterpret the passages that necessitate a "near" or
"soon" fulfillment of the particular prophecy. This can
be seen in the numerous twists that have been done to
the exegesis of Matthew 24:34. Most either try (poorly)
to reinterpret "this generation" as "this race," or they
will say "all these things" only refers to some of the
verses previous to the statement but not "*all*" of them
(like the verse says). A similar instance is the slippery
means by which people try to avoid the "soon" statements in the book of Revelation. The predetermined
grid they are trying to fit everything into says these
passages must be referring to the Final Advent of Christ;
therefore, they do all they can to ensure that they are
viewed that way.

Each passage must be interpreted in its own context. The comparison of other Scripture passages for
help in interpretating "nearness" only extends to passages of similar context; we cannot assume a passage
that does not mention nearness is implying it, unless
we have biblical justification.

The New Testament is not the only place in Scripture that speaks of the fulfillment of prophecy as being
"near" (contrary to the way that pantelists make it appear). There are a number of places in the prophets
that foretell events that are to come soon, and these are
critical for our present discussion. It appears as though
the pantelist has been happy to apply his "universal
hermeneutic" (i.e., if one passage says "near" then everything is near) to the New Testament without thinking about the nightmare he would find himself in if he
applied it equally as firmly to the Old Testament.

In fact the very first prophecy in the Bible had an
extremely long-term fulfillment. In Genesis 3:15, after
the fall, God promises the coming of Christ, which did
not take place (by the shortest possible reckoning) for
another four thousand years. In addition, it appears that

Adam and Eve thought the fulfillment of the prophecy
was going to be "near" (since "Cain" means "gotten,"
Eve's exclamation in 4:1 reveals that she thought Cain
was the one who would crush the head of the serpent),
yet they were wrong. We notice, however, that God
said "your seed" (3:15), and thus Eve was mistaken in
assuming it was to be her *first* seed, rather than her seed
that was to come thousands of years later! According
to pantelist exegesis, this is exactly what Eve should
have thought. The error here needs no further explanation.

Let us look at a few more passages in this regard
that are found in Isaiah:

> For in a very little while my indignation will come to an end,
> and my anger will be directed to their destruction. (10:25)

> Wail, for the day of the Lord is near; as destruction from
> the Almighty it will come. (13:6)

> Hyenas will cry in its towers, and jackals in the pleasant
> palaces; its time is close at hand and its days will not be
> prolonged. (13:22)

Isaiah, writing around the mid-seventh century, said
that both the destruction of Jerusalem and of Israel's
enemies was near. The first deportation was only around
forty years later, and the final destruction itself came
in 586 B.C. Much of what Isaiah wrote about discusses
this war in detail (so much detail that liberal theologians often date its writing after the actual events).

The destruction of Jerusalem in 586 B.C. is not, however, his only topic. Isaiah also discusses the coming of
the Messiah. In chapter nine Isaiah tells about the ascension of Christ into heaven, where He sat down at
the right hand of the Father (9:6–7).[17] In chapter eleven
he speaks about the coming of Christ, "the branch" "from
the stump of Jesse" (11:1).[18] And then later in chapter

fifty-three, Isaiah tells of Jesus' death on the cross. These
(and other) passages speak of events that the Church
unanimously believes happened in the first century in
the life, death, and resurrection of Jesus Christ (this is
what makes us Christian). Notice that the fulfillment
of the passages that foretell the coming of Christ did
not come about until over six hundred years after Isaiah
gave the prophecy. Would anyone dare to refer to this
as "near?" It would make just as much a mockery of
the "near" references in Isaiah as we currently see
dispensationalism doing to the "near" references in the
New Testament. Daniel, writing some hundred years
after Isaiah, was told that his prophecies of the coming
of Christ (which took place five hundred years later)
were not near (8:16–26). How could we possibly say
the prophecies in Isaiah of the coming of Christ were
"near" when they were given even earlier than Daniel's
prophecies? According to pantelism, though, this is what
the Jews *should* have believed about the Messiah.

Isaiah is not the only prophet to do this. Jeremiah
48:16 accurately foretells the destruction of Moab by
Nebuchadnezzar by saying: "The calamity of Moab is
near at hand and his affliction hastens apace." Does this
"nearness" necessitate that every prophecy in Jeremiah
is "near" also? If so, then the coming of the New Covenant prophesied in Jeremiah 31:31ff must have happened in the sixth century B.C. rather than at the last
supper (Luke 22:20).

Ezekiel also has numerous references to "nearness."

> But say to them, "The days are at hand, and the fulfillment
> of *every* vision" (12:23; emphasis added).

> You have become guilty by the blood which you have shed,
> and defiled by the idols which you have made; and you have
> brought your day near, the appointed time of your years has
> come. (22:4)

Wail, "Alas for the day!" For the day is near, the day of the Lord is near; it will be a day of clouds, a time of doom for the nations. (30:2–3)

We find the same idea here as in Isaiah and Jeremiah. Do these "near" passages make all prophecies in Ezekiel also near? If the original readers of the prophets expected these things to come soon, then according to pantelism they should have automatically expected everything the prophets said to come soon. If today someone were to take the passages of the Old Testament and change their meaning so they could say events did happen soon, even the pantelist would reject it, but this is the very thing the pantelists are doing with the New Testament. There are many prophecies in Ezekiel that did not come to fulfillment until the first century with the coming of Christ. Did the pouring out of the Holy Spirit in New Testament salvation (Ezek. 37:25–28) take place in the sixth century B.C. or in the first century A.D.? If the pantelist manner of interpretation is accepted as true, then we must affirm that all these things took place before the New Testament says they did.

There are many other "near" passages in the Old Testament (e.g., Joel 1:15; 2:1; 3:14; Zeph. 1:7; 1:14) that clearly are referring to events that took place "soon" after the prophecy was given (exactly as the verses said they would); to say otherwise would go against the clear testimony of the Scriptures. Yet this does not force us to say that all prophecies in the Old Testament were fulfilled soon, but only those that say so. If the pantelist is correct in his assumptions with respect to the New Testament, then this same exegesis must be used for the Old Testament.

This would mean that Christ sat down at the right hand of God (Dan. 7:13f) before He was born as a man, and Christ accomplished salvation (Dan. 9:24f) before He was crucified. This obviously makes a complete mockery of the prophecies found in Scripture. If, however, this exegetical method does not work in the Old Testament (and we have seen that it does not) then what justification do we have for applying it to the New Testament? The answer is clear: we have no justification for the exegetical assumption of pantelism. This is possibly the most fatal flaw of pantelism: it doesn't fit with the rest of Scripture.

The texts in the Old Testament (and thus the New Testament as well) that have a clear reference to "nearness" and historical connections for their fulfillment were undoubtedly fulfilled at that time. The texts, however, have no "nearness" note (such as those that refer to the first coming of Christ in the Old Testament, and those which refer to the Final Advent in the New Testament) and should not be forced to fit into a "near" context. They should be accepted as such only if their context clearly denotes it as such. Our application for the New Testament should be clear. If a text says something is "near," then we must accept it as true. If, however, the text does not make any reference to "nearness," we must not assume it is controlled by the "near" statements found elsewhere and thus seek to interpret it as having happened in the past. The pantelists attempt to say that Scripture interprets Scripture, yet they are radically inconsistent with that method of interpretation, for they do not apply it to the Old Testament.

*Notes:*

[1] See Deuteronomy 29:23; 32:32; Isaiah 1:10; 3:9; 13:19; Jeremiah 23:14; Lamentations 4:6; Ezekiel 16:46–49; Amos 4:11; Zephaniah 2:9; 2 Peter 2:6; and Jude 7.

[2] See Russell, *Parousia*, p. 206ff.

[3] The words used are the standard verbs for physical resurrection in other contexts: ἀνίστημι and ἐγείρω. See Matthew 20:19; John 6:40; 11:23; 1 Thessalonians 4:14; Matthew 10:8; 16:21; 28:6; John 2:22; 12:1; Romans 6:4; 1 Corinthians 15:4; 15:52; 1 Peter 1:21; etc.

[4] μετά τῆς γενεᾶς ταύτης—μετά is defined by *BAG* as "with, among, in company with someone," p. 508.

[5] Christ reigns over unbelievers too; that is just not Paul's topic here. It is impossible to make "living and dead" in verse nine refer to believers (spiritually living) and unbelievers (spiritually dead) because the entire context is dealing with believers' relations to one another.

[6] Pantelists want to say that all usages of μέλλω are proof of a "soon-coming" reference. Though Paul does use μέλλω in verse one, this word does not always mean "about to," see *BAG*, p. 501.

[7] This is the situation we find often with pantelism. The pantelist wants every word in the Bible to always have the same meaning regardless of context or what the rest of Scripture says. The instance we are examining here, the relation of 1 John 4:17 to John 5:24f, is a clear example of how impossible this is.

[8] Notice how Paul, in Romans 8 uses κατακρίνω, which means specifically "condemn" and not κρίνω, which refers to "judgment" in general, whether good or bad.

[9] See Crews, David P., *Prophecy Fullfilled* (Austin, TX: New Light Publishing, 1994), p. 311.

[10] βασανίζω.

[11] καιρός often carries an eschatological connotation (See *BAG*, p. 395).

[12] φυλακή

[13] John uses βασανίζω here to describe the eternal torment; the same word is used in Matthew 8:29 by the demon who knew his time for torment had not yet come.

[14] This word, which occurs only once in the New Testament, is from ταρταρόω "hold captive in Tartarus" (*BAG*, p. 805). Tartarus was the temporary ancient abode of the dead where punishment was meted out.

[15] ἐστιν must be assumed in the text; John does not give it. He thus assumes they "were" or "are" already in the lake of fire. In order to equate the times of their punishment he would have had to supply some form of verb.

[16] Fadeley, Gene, *Revelation: Kingdoms in Conflict* (Charlotte,

NC: Anchor Publishing, 1995) says "The only power Satan can have in our lives is what we voluntarily give him. Without us, he can do nothing. Satan is powerless. Satan had been released but he was severely defeated" (p. 73). This would be fine were he describing Satan in the abyss waiting for judgment, but he is describing Satan (whom he thinks is) already punished and in hell. This is a ridiculous truncating of the doctrine of eternal punishment. Further, he entirely avoids discussing when Satan was "already bound" and when he was "released." Fadeley has created a Satan that was never really bound, and therefore never released; he has now been eternally punished so poorly that he can still influence this world by the mere desire of fallen men. God's punishment of Satan (by Fadeley's description) has had little effect on this world.

[17] No, this passage does *not* speak about the birth of Christ; it speaks about His heavenly coronation. He did not sit "upon the throne of David" (9:7) at His birth; it was after He ascended into heaven.

[18] Notice how these references are right in amongst the context of the "near" passages quoted above. The order cannot be mistaken: Isaiah 9:6 (A.D. 30); 10:25 (sixth century B.C.); 11:1 (A.D. 30); 13:6; and 13:22 (sixth century B.C.). Isaiah clearly moves back and forth between "near" events and "far" events, yet the "near" events do not force the "far" events to be near as well. If Isaiah could do it here, couldn't Paul in 1 Thessalonians 4:13–5:11?

**Chapter Five**

# The Resurrection

OF ALL THE TOPICS THE PANTELISTS HAVE REWORKED, THE most difficult one is what is called the "general resurrection."[1] Numerous passages make reference to the general resurrection of all men at the end of time. Although I do not have the space to give a detailed exposition of every one of those passages, I will spend a good deal of time on the primary passages. Even if there were only one passage in all of Scripture that taught the physical resurrection of all men, that would be enough. This is not the case we are dealing with though; there is a wealth of passages that proves the orthodox understanding of the resurrection. We will not focus on the many different opinions among pantelists regarding the interpretation of the resurrection—there are too many of them to respond to each one individually—but I will speak to some of the most common interpretations put forward by pantelism.

### The Death of Death
Some three hundred years ago, John Owen wrote a magnificent treatise with the title: "The Death of Death in the Death of Christ." This work (which has never been sufficiently responded to) displays conclusively how on the cross, Christ completely conquered "death." Death was not merely injured or slowed down but conquered. Owen meant that Christ was the complete vic-

tor over everything that could in any way hinder the salvation of the children of God. Although numerous passages in the New Testament support this glorious truth, there are also some passages that look similar but actually discuss an entirely different event than Owen was speaking of. Let us look at a few of these references:

> The last enemy to be destroyed is death. (1 Cor. 15:26)

> When the perishable puts on the imperishable, and the mortal puts on immortality, then shall come to pass the saying that is written: "Death is swallowed up in victory." (1 Cor. 15:54)

> Then Death and Hades were thrown into the lake of fire. (Rev. 20:14)

Each of these passages speaks of an event that is future to the writer, whether one is pantelist, preterist, or any other position. In 1 Corinthians, Paul taught that at some day in his future, "Death" was going to be "destroyed" and "swallowed up in victory." In the book of Revelation, John taught that at some day in his future, "Death" (along with Hades) was going to be conquered and thrown into hell. These verses must be compared with others that refer to death having been conquered on the cross. You see, if the New Testament authors believed that death *was* conquered and also that death *will be* conquered, they were either contradicting themselves or they were referring to two different things:

> He who hears my word and believes . . . has passed from death to life. (John 5:24)

> Yield yourselves to God as men who have been brought from death to life. (Rom. 6:13)

> And you he made alive, when you were dead through the trespasses and sins in which you once walked. (Eph. 2:1–2)

> ... Christ Jesus, who abolished death and brought life and immortality to light through the gospel. (2 Tim. 1:10)

> We know that we have passed out of death into life. (1 Jn. 3:14)

These verses speak of how believers, here in this life, pass from death to life. This is something that had already happened for the Christians of the first century. They were not waiting for this to occur. Whatever Paul meant by saying that "the last enemy to be destroyed is death" (1 Cor. 15:26), it was not the same thing as the spiritual regeneration that had already come to the people of God. Pantelists often claim that the "death" that was to be destroyed was "sin-death,"[2] or the state of being spiritually dead because of one's sin. If this is true, then Paul believed he and other Christians both *had been* delivered from their sins (as in Eph. 2:1) and *would be* delivered from their sins (1 Cor. 15:26). Unfortunately one cannot have it both ways. The deliverance from sins (which Paul calls "life from death") was past; the deliverance from mortality (which Paul calls "resurrection") was future. He is not speaking of the same event.

What "death" therefore was conquered in A.D. 70? Max King and others connect this "death" with the nation of Israel. They claim Israel was in a state of "sin-death" as a nation and that the resurrection was the promised deliverance from that state of "sin-death." This *sounds* nice and biblical, but it is not. It would be fantastic if we could look back and see that the nation (or at least a large majority of it) was delivered from its "sin-death" in A.D. 70 (according to King's explanation of Rom. 11:26). However, one of the fundamental points in preterist (and pantelist) interpretation is that the nation of Israel remained apostate (proportionately few Jews

were saved in the first century—Rom. 11:5). We cannot have both: either the nation was saved and delivered from her "sin-death" in 70, or she was condemned
and rejected. History (in addition to the prophecies of
the New Testament) records that Israel was condemned.
There is nothing in history that corresponds to a "deliverance" of the nation of Israel from "death to life."

If, however, pantelists say that Israel was the Old
Israel being resurrected in the form of the New Israel,
who was delivered from her "sin-death" in the convert-
ing of many Jews to Christ in the first century, then
once again we have a serious dilemma. If "sin-death"
denotes a state of spiritual death as a result of one's sin,
then this was not "completed" in A.D. 70, for people
(including those who still say they are ethnically Jewish) have been coming to Christ (and thus released from
their "sin-death") for two thousand years now. This was
certainly not something completed (or begun) in A.D.
70. It is still going on today. In addition, what is different between now and the period between A.D. 30 and
70? People still come to Christ, and once in Christ,
people still sin. Merely saying it is different because
one's interpretation of the Bible says it is different does
not make it so. The pantelist is hard pressed to come
up with a way that our state of salvation is different
from Paul's (and thus also prove that the last two thousand years of sin is actually a complete and perfect deliverance from the state of sin).

When Paul, in Romans 11, says that Israel's acceptance means "life from the dead" (Rom. 11:15), he means
the same thing he referred to in Ephesians 2:1 above:
spiritual life from spiritual death. This is why a few verses
later his description of their coming back into the people
of God is grounded in whether they "persist in their
unbelief" (11:23). Israel does not get saved from "sin-
death" merely because she is Jewish, but only if she
believes. The reference to Christ saving Israel in 11:26

refers to His death on the cross (which they needed to have faith in). The reference in 11:27 refers to the New Covenant He made the night before His death. Israel's "life from the dead" is exactly the same "life from death" that is experienced by all believers. The context of this passage shows that Paul is speaking about his desire for the salvation of souls (see Rom. 10:1; 10:9; 10:17; 11:6; 11:11; 11:14; 11:23; 11:28). To try to make "life from the dead" mean a national deliverance from "sin-death" must be brought into the passage from the outside. Paul is clearly speaking about the individual salvation of repentant Israelites.

What therefore can we gather from this? Christians experience the conquering of spiritual death at their conversion. Christ (who was never spiritually dead) experienced the conquering of physical death when He was resurrected. The only death left for us to experience being conquered is the death of our physical bodies, exactly as Christ Himself experienced already. Christ draws us to Himself in our spiritual conversion, wherein we experience eternal spiritual life. The only thing left that Paul (and the other authors of the New Testament) could have been waiting for was a physical "life from death."

### Resurrection from Sin?

The contention that the resurrection Paul awaited was a spiritual resurrection from "sin-death" must be examined further. I do not wish in any way to make it seem as though I deny that the Scriptures use the idea of "death" to describe the state of being fallen in sin. This, however, does not mean that every time we find the use of the word "death," it is referring to spiritual death (as in 1 Cor. 15:3–4), or every time we find the use of the word "sin," it is referring to spiritual death (as in 1 Jn. 2:1).

From the very beginning of the Bible, we find the

usage of "death" to refer to the state of being fallen in sin. In Genesis 2:17, Adam is told that if he disobeys God he "shall die." The primary reference here is not to physical death (or else it would be wrong since Adam died hundreds of years later). God is telling Adam his soul and his body would "die" (*both* in a figurative sense). His soul became spiritually dead (turned away from God), and his body "died" in that it fell from its state of perfection (he was now subject to disease, sickness, and physical death), and thus physical death is a result of spiritual death. It is not the same thing (Rom. 5:12).[3] The comparison between Adam's physical state before the fall and after is clearly described as "life and death." Though all of this is true, we find that the idea of "death" extends beyond the concept of spiritual death to physical death[4] (which is the final outcome of sin—Rom. 5:12).

Therefore we seek to answer the question of whether the Scriptures distinguish between resurrection from sin and resurrection from physical death. In asking this question, it should already be obvious that there must be some manner of distinction. If there were not, we would be forced to say that the stories of Lazarus, Jairus's daughter, and others were merely parables and that Jesus Himself was delivered from His sinfulness! Pantelists do not, however, assert these things, and therefore we have a starting point to define how we are to distinguish between physical resurrection and spiritual resurrection.[5]

Let us first look at the "uncontested" passages regarding physical resurrection:

> "O Lord my God, let this child's soul come into him again."
> And the Lord hearkened to the voice of Elijah; and the soul of the child came into him again, and he revived.
> (1 Kgs. 17:21–22)

> When Elisha came into the house, he saw the child lying dead on his bed. So he went in and shut the door upon the two of

them, and prayed to the Lord . . . [and] the flesh of the child became warm . . . and the child opened his eyes. (2 Kgs. 4:32–35)

A man was being buried . . . and the man was cast into the grave of Elisha; and as soon as the man touched the bones of Elisha, he revived, and stood on his feet. (2 Kgs. 13:21)

The tombs also were opened, and many bodies of the saints who had fallen asleep were raised, and coming out of the tombs after [Christ's] resurrection they went into the holy city and appeared to many. (Matt. 27:52–53)

And he said "Young man, I say to you, arise." And the dead man sat up, and began to speak. (Luke 7:14–15)

But taking her by the hand he called, saying, "Child, arise." And her spirit returned, and she got up at once. (Luke 8:54–55)

He cried with a loud voice, "Lazarus, come out." The dead man came out. (John 11:43–44)

In those days she fell sick and died. . . . But Peter put them all outside and knelt down and prayed; then turning to the body he said, "Tabitha, rise." . . . And he gave her his hand and lifted her up. Then calling the saints and widows he presented her alive. (Acts 9:37, 40–41)

He fell down from the third story and was taken up dead. But Paul went down and bent over him. . . . And they took the lad away alive. (Acts 20:9–12)

What do we find here in these numerous passages? Each of them makes it clear that the person spoken of was dead, not merely injured. Each of them uses standard terms about a person's "body" being "dead" and show that afterward they were definitely alive, some even going so far as to point out that the "spirit" returned to the body (thus making it clear that the person was physically dead—see James 2:26).

With this being a well-known type of event for the early Church, we would expect the authors of the New Testament to clearly differentiate between physical resurrection and some form of spiritual resurrection. Paul does speak of a resurrection "from the dead" that is clearly not a physical resurrection. In Ephesians 2:1 Paul says we were "made alive when you were dead through the trespasses and sins." His qualification here is clear. The "death" he is speaking of is a spiritual death that results from sin and not physical death. Again in verse five of the same chapter, he uses the same image with the same qualification. His point is clear: a life lived in sin is "dead" when compared to a life lived in righteousness. He also uses this idea in Colossians 2:13 where he says, "You, who were dead in trespasses . . . God made alive." His reference to "death" is once again qualified by "trespasses." Something we must note here is that this idea of spiritual resurrection is a *past* event for Paul and his readers. They are not waiting for this to occur, nor does he say it is a process that began in the past. In various places, Paul describes the glories of the Christian life as one's having been "brought from death to life" (Rom. 6:13), but the context is always a "death" of sinful fallen man, and the "life" is always the present life of being with Christ.

When Paul speaks of the anticipated resurrection, there is a marked absence of references to sin. The following passages (which I hold to be speaking of the physical resurrection) are without a reference to sin or sin as death: Matthew 22:23–32; Luke 14:12–14; 20:27–39; John 6:39–40, 44, 54; Acts 24:14–15; 26:4–8; Romans 8:18–29; 1 Corinthians 15:12–55[6]; 2 Corinthians 4:13–5:10[7]; Philippians 3:7–21; 1 Thessalonians 4:13–18; Hebrews 11:35. There are also a few passages that do make reference to "sin" and "death as sin" that I believe are referring to physical resurrection that need to be looked at briefly now.

In the first of these, John 5:25–29, Jesus says the "dead" will hear his voice and live. It is clear from the context that He is speaking of the spiritual regeneration that happens to every believer at conversion. In addition, He contrasts the "dead" coming to life with those who "are in the tombs" (5:28) who come to life. It is clear our Lord is speaking of two different things here. However we interpret them, it is obvious He distinguishes between them (the first "now is" and the second "is coming"). It is no accident that He says the first group of people are "dead" and the second group are "in the tombs." Jesus wants us to see that the second group is clearly referring to those who are physically dead ("in the tombs"). Thus the "death" in 5:25 is a spiritual death, but Jesus discriminates between these two types of "death." Some have tried to say this distinction displays a process of "spiritual resurrection."[8] There is nothing within this passage or any other that denotes that resurrection is a process. This is an example of the pantelist grasping at straws.

In Romans 8:5–8, Paul speaks about the state of those who are "in the flesh" and says that this state is "death." Then in 8:9–11 he discusses the "resurrection." Verse 11 says, "[H]e who raised Christ Jesus from the dead will give life to your mortal bodies." Some pantelists assume the references to spiritual death in 8:5–8 control the references to resurrection in 8:9–11. Were we, however, to make this assumption, we would need to ignore what the passage itself says. Paul says his readers were "not in the flesh" but were rather "in the Spirit" (8:9), which means our "spirits are alive" (8:10). And if this is true, then "he . . . will give life to your mortal bodies" (8:11). Paul here assumes his readers are already alive spiritually and that it is their bodies that need revivification "because of sin." Thus we can ask, if this "resurrection" occurred for all believers in the first century, why do Christians still sin? And if we still sin, what has this "resurrection" accomplished for us? According to the pantelist, Christians' bodies were dead because of sin, and they are now alive, but they still sin. Would not the continuing sin cause them to die again? After all, we aren't yet free of the effects of the fall. It is clear that Paul is not speaking here of an event that is spiritual; rather he means a receiving of "life" in the "mortal body" that will deliver it not only from the effects of the fall but also from ever dying again.

The last passage that has "sin" in it is 1 Corinthians 6:12–20. We believe Paul's statement (though short)[9] in verse fourteen, "God raised the Lord and will also raise us up by his power," is referring to a future (to us) physical resurrection at the end of time. The reason Paul speaks of sin here is clear. He is telling the Corinthian believers their bodies should not be used for evil but rather for righteousness. Our bodies are destined for the glory of God (6:20) at the present time as well as in the future when they will be raised (6:14). Therefore since they will someday be raised to glory, we should live now in the same holiness that we will someday participate in.

The concept of resurrection from sin in the New Testament is not nearly as prevalent as the concept of resurrection from the dead. Though the ideas of "sin" and "death" are often related, we cannot assume from this that they are always the same thing. Scripture clearly speaks at times of a physical resurrection (such as Lazarus); therefore the concept was known by the early Church. We would be just as wrong if we assumed every reference to "life from death" meant physical resurrection as the pantelists are in assuming that these references mean a spiritual resurrection. In fact the only way the authors of the New Testament were able to ever use the metaphor of "life from death" to describe a spiritual transformation was because they knew there was a physical reality that corresponded to it. At the very least, the temporary resurrections of Lazarus and others must be seen as related to the concept of spiritual "life from death." The authors of the New Testament clearly differentiated between physical and spiritual resurrection (as seen above) because the physical resurrections that had already occurred were a potential for confusion in this concept. When they spoke of physical resurrection, they used the terms that are used for the "undisputed" resurrections in order to show that they were speaking of the same type of event.

If we can see in certain passages that the idea of "resurrection" can refer to either a physical temporary resurrection (as with Lazarus), a physical permanent resurrection (as with Christ), or a spiritual resurrection that takes place at conversion (as in Eph 2:1), then what criteria do we use to distinguish what is being spoken of?[10] Even the pantelist must have some criteria for this. There is basic agreement in regard to the physical resurrections done by the prophets, apostles, and Christ Himself, as well as about Christ's own resurrection. The main point of contention comes in relation to the passages that describe a resurrection the apostles were waiting for. Was it similar to the "resurrection" of regeneration, of Lazarus (and thus physical but temporary), or of Christ (and thus physical but permanent)?[11] Numerous references throughout Scripture have traditionally been taken to refer to the physical resurrection at the end of this world. I will next examine a few of these to see if there is any support for pantelism.

### Matthew 10

In Matthew 10 we find a curious reference that causes severe difficulties for the denial of the physical resurrection. The context of the passage is as follows:

> So have no fear of them; for nothing is covered that will not be revealed, or hidden that will not be known. What I tell you

in the dark, utter in the light; and what you hear whispered, proclaim upon the housetops. And do not fear those who kill the body but cannot kill the soul; rather fear him who can destroy both soul and body in hell. (Matt. 10:26–28)

Clearly, Jesus is speaking in a context of judgment. As he says later in verse thirty-two, those who refuse to "acknowledge" Christ before men will be punished for it. From this alone we cannot tell if He is speaking of temporal or eternal judgment. It is the statement in verse twenty-eight that not only helps to determine this but also causes such difficulty for the pantelist. There Jesus warns the disciples not to be afraid of someone who can only "kill the body but cannot kill the soul." They are those who would persecute the Church that Jesus referred to earlier in the same passage (10:21–23).

The word Jesus uses for "kill"[12] is the most common Greek word used in the New Testament for "killing" and has no special nuances. When, however, Jesus tells the disciples to "fear him who can destroy both soul and body in hell," He changes the word; He does not say "kill" but "destroy."[13] The change of wording here is significant because Jesus is clearly not referring to an ordinary ending of life (as with those who "kill the body") but something that is much worse (such that Jesus would tell them to "fear him"). In fact, this word carries the connotation of "ruin, destroy" or "lose."[14] In addition, Jesus uses the word twice in Matthew 10:39 where (with the word translated as "lose") He says "he who finds his life will lose it, and he who loses his life for my sake will find it." Clearly here the word does not mean merely to "die," because all men die, and thus His distinction here would be meaningless. Also, we can see that it cannot mean to "be killed" because Jesus already said that many of the faithful (i.e., those who "lose their life for Christ's sake") will be killed (10:21).

What conclusions can we make here? Jesus tells the disciples to not be afraid of their persecutors (who can merely kill them) but to be afraid of God Almighty who can send them to eternal hell. This is where the difficulty comes in for the pantelist. When God sends someone to hell, it is not (according to Jesus Himself) merely the soul that is sent but "soul and body." Now if the condemned are sent to hell *after* death, then what body is it that they are sent there with? The pantelist would say that our bodies are not physically resurrected, and therefore the experience of hell (and heaven) is merely a spiritual experience. Our bodies are dead and buried never to rise again. How, we must ask, does He send the body to hell if it is dead and buried? Unless He were to make those who "sleep in the dust of the earth" (clearly referring to the physical death and burial of the body) "awake" (Dan. 12:2), it would be impossible. Without mentioning any reference to a national resurrection (as per many pantelists), Jesus clearly assumes that when people are sent to hell they are sent there "both soul and body," and thus it is not merely a spiritual suffering in hell but a physical experience as well.

### Luke 20
Various references in the Scriptures point out how the Pharisees believed in the "resurrection," whereas the Sadducees did not (see e.g., Acts 23:8). However we interpret the "resurrection," this point is clear. Whether to view it as a "national resurrection"[15] or as a "symbolic . . . *rising* to a state of vindication"[16] or as a physical rising of dead bodies, this was one of their basic disagreements. Thus we find in Luke 20 a situation where the Sadducees are testing Jesus to see whether He agrees with them or the Pharisees. After giving a story about a woman who had seven successive husbands (in obedience to Mosaic Law), the Sadducees ask Jesus, "In the resurrection, therefore, whose wife will the woman be? For the seven had her as wife" (Luke 20:33).

The first thing we must tackle here is the nature of

the Sadducees' question: were they denying a physical
resurrection or some other form that the pantelists would
affirm? The text is quite clear as to the nature of what
the Sadducees were saying. In fact they seem to go out
of their way to point out what it was that they didn't
believe.

First, their question involved a situation after the
physical death of the individuals involved (20:31–32).
Secondly, if conjugal rights were not the issue with the
Sadducees' concept of "post-resurrection marriage," then
there would be no concern for "whose wife" she would
be. Therefore they were assuming the "resurrection"
state was physical. If they were asking about a "national
revival/resurrection" or a "symbolic" resurrection, then
there would be little concern for those who had physically died. If we insert the pantelist assumptions into
the Sadducees' question, then their question makes no
sense at all. Thus we must assume here that they were
asking about a resurrection that involved physical bodies coming back to life.

If this is so, and there is no reason in the text to
assume otherwise, then why did Jesus only correct them
on the issue of marriage? Why did He not also show
them that the resurrection was not something physical? He clearly supports the "resurrection from the dead,"
which they were denying, in His answer (20:35–37).
Additionally, it cannot be said that Jesus was only de-
fending physical resurrection here because He was to
be resurrected. In His statement "the dead are raised"
(20:37), He uses a plural form of the word "dead." This
would be rendered literally "those who are dead are
raised."

Jesus' description of those who are resurrected is
remarkable. He says that "those who are accounted
worthy to attain to that age and to the resurrection from
the dead . . . cannot die any more, because they are
equal to angels and are sons of God, being sons of the

resurrection" (20:35–36). The reference to "that age" is most probably referring to the "age" in which the resurrection takes place. This would be the "age to come" referred to throughout the Scriptures—our present age. It is in this age that the resurrection happens. There is no clue in the text to refer to when the resurrection occurs (whether at the beginning or at the end). It merely says that it is in connection to "that age." In fact, Jesus does not even say "you who are accounted worthy" but "those who are accounted worthy" (literally "the ones accounted worthy"), thus allowing for it to be people who are not yet alive when Jesus was speaking.[17]

Jesus' description that they are not able to "die any more" is what is most fascinating. What is the context of "dying" in the passage? Clearly, the only dying referred to involves the seven men and one woman who died (physically) that the Sadducees were asking about (20:31–32), and thus when Jesus says "cannot die any more"[18] (20:36), what type of "dying" is it that cannot happen "any more"? It must be physical death that He is referring to, since anything else must be inserted into the text. When Jesus says these people are "equal to angels," He does not mean that they are without physical bodies, for He does not say that in the text anywhere. In what sense are they "equal to angels"? They are "equal" in that the angels live forever in their current state (they "cannot die"); so too, those who are resurrected "cannot die any more." In their resurrected physical bodies they will live forever.[19]

In Jesus' answer He says that in the resurrection people "neither marry nor are given in marriage" (20:35). An appeal to 1 Corinthians 7:29[20] as the reason for this statement is not only a stretch (by connecting two unrelated passages), but it is also impossible. Paul said "let those who have wives live as though they had none" (1 Cor. 7:29) as a rule for the "present distress" (7:26) that existed *before* A.D. 70. In other words, Paul gave this guideline for life *until* the coming of Christ in 70, whereas the statement Jesus makes in Luke 20:35 is regarding life *after* His coming in 70. This once again shows how the pantelists will ignore the context of a passage (sometimes even a clear preterist context) in order to support their system.

Jesus does not say that those who are resurrected "are like those who are neither married nor given in marriage" but that they are "not married." Additionally, what does Jesus say is the reason they aren't given in marriage? He says "for they cannot die anymore" (20:36).[21] The purpose of marriage was temporary— for this life alone, and for the primary purpose of bringing about a "godly offspring" (Mal. 2:15). In the resurrection state, there is no longer any need for marriage, at least in the exact form known now.

One last issue must be covered here. At the end of Jesus' discussion, the scribes state that they agree with Jesus (20:39). They were convinced by what He said. Yet if Jesus was only teaching them about some sort of "rising to vindication before God" or a "national resurrection," then why did the Sadducees disagree with them? Even in the first five books of the Bible (which were all that the Sadducees held to), it can be seen that God vindicates those who are His (Ex. 2:23–25; 9:16; 14:4) and that He would restore His nation when they were faithful (Deut. 28:13; 30:1–5). Yet if they denied the spiritual realm and the physical resurrection of dead bodies (Acts 23:8), then the discussion here is clear. There is no other option in this passage.

### John 5 and 6

These passages are some of the clearest references to the Final Resurrection in the New Testament. Jesus says in John 5:

> Truly, truly, I say to you, he who hears my word and believes him who sent me, has eternal life; he does not come into

judgment, but has passed from death to life. Truly, truly I
say to you, the hour is coming, and now is, when the dead
will hear the voice of the Son of God, and those who hear will
live.... Do not marvel at this; for the hour is coming when
all who are in the tombs will hear his voice and come forth,
those who have done good, to the resurrection of life, and
those who have done evil, to the resurrection of judgment.
(John 5:24–29)

It is apparent to even the most casual observer that Jesus
is making some sort of distinction between the "dead"
hearing His voice and the "living," and "all who are in
the tombs . . . coming forth." Let us look at the specific
distinctions that our Lord makes here.

First, He says the "dead coming to life" is something that was not only future but was already present.
In comparison, He says that those "coming forth out
of the tombs" was something that was "coming" but
not yet present. One was present, the other was future. How far in the future is not clear from the context.

Second, Jesus says that the "dead" who "live" are
only doing so as a result of a condition: "those who
hear will live." It is not all the "dead" who live but only
"those who hear." The close connection He makes between personal salvation in verse twenty-four ("he who
believes me") and the "dead" coming to "life" in verse
twenty-five makes it clear that they are speaking of the
same thing. "Those who hear [and accept the gospel]
will live." Whereas in the second group it is "*all*" who
are in the tombs" that hear "his voice."[22] It is not merely
some but *all* that "come forth" from their tombs. Therefore, we cannot say that Jesus is referring to just Israel, or just believers; He clearly says "all" who are in
their tombs.

Third, those who are "dead" are said merely to "live."
Thus one state exists for all those who are "dead" with
no distinctions. In the second situation, however, we

see that even though "all" come forth from their tombs, not all have the same destiny. Some "come forth" to "life" while others come forth to "judgment."

Although Jesus is using similar images (the dead coming back to life), it is clear that He is differentiating between them. He does not want us to confuse the two nor think that they are merely two parts of the same thing; they have different subjects, different results, and different time frames. The "eternal life" that exists for those in verse twenty-five is a present reality ("has eternal life," vs. 24). The "eternal life" that exists for those in verse twenty-eight is a future reality.[23]

The association with the many references to a future "raising" of people found in chapter six of John also adds to this idea. We see in various places that Jesus says He will (in the future) raise those who are His own:

> I should lose nothing of all that he has given me, but raise it up at the last day. For this is the will of my Father, that every one who sees the Son and believes in him should have eternal life; and I will raise him up at the last day. (John 6:39–40)

> No one can come to me unless the Father who sent me draws him; and I will raise him up at the last day. (John 6:44)

> He who eats my flesh and drinks my blood has eternal life, and I will raise him up at the last day. (John 6:54)

There is no reason within the texts themselves to necessitate that this is referring to the "last day" of the Jewish age (unless one has predetermined that this is the meaning). The burden of proof is once again on the pantelist to show that these are not speaking of a physical raising of dead bodies to eternal resurrection life.

Finally, we must note here that if "all who are in the tombs" are resurrected, then this is an event after which there would be no one left in the tombs. All graves would be empty (has anything even remotely like this ever happened?). Of course the pantelist will here attempt to make the resurrection some sort of nonphysical event. If, however, "those who have done evil" are a nonphysically dead group of people then they will be resurrected to more nonphysical deadness. Thus they are raised to death (and thus unaffected by this event). Does this make sense? Jesus' usage of "resurrection to life" does not mean that the resurrection will make them alive (that's redundant—the idea of life is inherent in the word "resurrection"). It means they will have the fullest capacity of life, both physically and spiritually, in God's glorious presence forever.

"Resurrection to judgment" means they will be "alive" physically, but it will not be blessed life. Because they will be enduring judgment for all eternity, their resurrection is truly a resurrection unto judgment. The pantelist says the resurrection for "those who have done evil" does not bring them into physical life; rather they are resurrected from being a disembodied spirit to being a (still) disembodied spirit. What purpose does this have? None. Thus we are again drawn to acknowledge that the resurrection is the reviving of physically dead bodies that have their original souls returned to them for all eternity, and this will take place on the "Last Day."

### John 11

The resurrection of Lazarus in John 11 is possibly the most dramatic of all of Jesus' miracles. Not only was Lazarus dead, he also had been buried for four days. It may have been possible for skeptics to deny some of Jesus' previous miracles, but this one was clear and indisputable. In addition, the references to the Final Resurrection are so powerful in this passage that they almost, by themselves, refute pantelism. Pantelists themselves have great difficulty with the statements made in John

11. Sometimes they apply the Lord's statements to vague generalities,[24] other times they ignore the context and assert that Jesus was referring only to spiritual resurrection,[25] or they assume that because the phrase "last day" is used in this context, it must mean the exact same thing as certain other texts that use "last" in their terminology.[26]

Let us examine here just what this passage reveals and see whether the suppositions of pantelism are found herein. The context of the passage is well known. Jesus hears of Lazarus's sickness and waits until he dies before He goes to him (11:1–15). Jesus specifically does this because He says it will show forth the glory of God (11:4). When Jesus arrives, Mary waits in the house while Martha immediately comes to speak to Him (11:20).

It is at this point that we begin to examine in detail the discussion that occurs. The section reads as follows:

> Martha said to Jesus, "Lord, if you had been here, my brother would not have died. And even now I know that whatever you ask from God, God will give you." Jesus said to her, "Your brother will rise again." Martha said to him, "I know that he will rise again in the resurrection at the last day." Jesus said to her, "I am the resurrection and the life; he who believes in me, though he die, yet shall he live, and whoever lives and believes in me shall never die. Do you believe this?" She said to him, "Yes, Lord; I believe that you are the Christ, the Son of God, he who is coming into the world." (John 11:21–27)

Martha tells Jesus she wants Lazarus back and that if Jesus had been there He could have healed him of his sickness in order to prevent him from dying (11:21). She then goes on to say that she has faith that Jesus can do anything (11:22); though she does not specifically ask Jesus to raise Lazarus's dead body to life, she may be hinting at it in this statement. Jesus Himself notices that this is what she is hinting at and responds to her in kind by affirming that Lazarus "will rise again." This statement, being a reference to something in the future, leads Martha to think that Jesus may have misunderstood her; she thought He was telling her Lazarus would "rise again" at the "last day" rather than at that moment (11:24). Affirming her faith in the "resurrection at the last day," Martha still hopes Jesus will do something for Lazarus right away. At this point we must ask, what was it Martha wanted Jesus to do? Her desire was obviously to have her brother alive again right then and there (even if we assume that the "last day resurrection" was an event in A.D. 70, that was still forty years distant and Martha wanted Lazarus to be with her right away).

Jesus does not correct Martha in her belief of a resurrection at the last day.[27] He rather gives her reason to have confidence about her place in that resurrection. When Jesus tells Martha He is the "resurrection and the life" (11:25), He defines specifically what the connection is that a person must have to enjoy that resurrection. He tells Martha, "He who believes in me, though he die, yet shall he live, and whoever lives and believes in me shall never die" (11:25–26). Here he makes a distinction between two things. We could paraphrase His statement by saying that "believers who die will live" and "believers who are alive will never die." I trust this paraphrase would be accepted by the pantelist (who would assume his own definitions for "live and die," as would we). What, however, do these two statements mean? Let us take both of these statements and compare them with others in Scripture.

Jesus says that the one who believes in Him and dies "shall live." What is this living that the believer will do? And when He says the believer who "lives" shall "never die," what is this living and dying that He is speaking of? To better understand the thrust of the

passage, let us view the two main phrases in parallel
fashion:

| (A) | (B) | (C) |
|-----|-----|-----|
| 1) he who believes in me | though he die | he shall live |
| 2) [he who] believes in me | [and] lives | shall never die |

The parallel under phrase (A) is clear. Jesus is speaking about true believers. On the other hand what we
find in (B) and (C) is an opposite rather than a parallel:
"die and live" and "live and die." When we examine them
closely though, we find that though the words "death"
and "life" are opposed to each other in this statement,
they are not referring to opposite ideas. It is apparent
that the "death" referred to is not the same in both verses.
In verse twenty-five "death" is assumed to be the experience of believers, whereas in verse twenty-six deliverance from "death" is promised for believers.
Additionally, the "living" is not spoken of in the same
way in these two verses; in verse twenty-five "living"
is spoken of as a promise for believers, whereas the
"living" in verse twenty-six is assumed as the experience of believers.[28]

Is Jesus saying in verse twenty-five that if a believer
(who thus has eternal life) dies spiritually he will be
spiritually resurrected? This does not make sense in
any system. The reference is clearly connected with
Lazarus in some fashion. He believed in Christ and died
and was about to be raised to life. But is this the only
reference Christ is making? He says "he who believes
in me," thus indicating a universal truth that applies to
all believers. But we know that not all believers experience a temporary raising from the dead as did Lazarus.
So what is Jesus referring to? The conclusion is actually quite simple. Jesus (Who *is* the resurrection Himself) will be the one to raise all men "at the last day,"
and He says He is giving a temporary example of that
raising "at the last day" as a foreshadowing of what it

will be like. The pantelist must recognize that the context of the specific passage we are dealing with is speaking about a physical raising of a man from the dead. We cannot ignore the obvious conclusions that would be made by those who heard Jesus say these things in this particular situation. Jesus didn't raise Lazarus just to show that He could. He was also teaching us about the "resurrection at the last day." If Jesus wanted to differentiate the "resurrection at the last day" from a physical resurrection, He picked quite a confusing miracle to perform in this context!

Jesus said that "he who believes in me" (meaning everyone who believes) "though he die" (a physical death like Lazarus, which comes to all men) "yet shall he live" (he will be raised from death in similar fashion to what you are about to see Me do to Lazarus). He is speaking here about the general resurrection as was already referred to in John 5:29. To attempt to make Jesus say here merely that believers who die physically will not experience the "death" of hell is to make the resurrection of Lazarus a confusing and deceptive counterpart to Jesus' teaching. Why would Jesus use the physical raising of a man from the dead to say that believers go to heaven? This would cause a great deal of confusion rather than clarity in the minds of those around.

The question that now must be answered about verse twenty-six is, What is the "living" that the believer is said to do there? There are various possibilities available. First, Jesus could be saying "the believer that has not yet died and is thus still alive, will never die." What would He mean by this though? Would Jesus be telling us that believers who haven't yet died, as Lazarus had, will never die, as Lazarus had? If so, He would be wrong.

Second, He could be saying that those who are alive spiritually will never die spiritually. This, however, is somewhat redundant and serves little purpose in the passage. Saying that those who are alive (spiritually) *and*

that they believe in Him is axiomatic and therefore su-
perfluous to the point He is making.

Third, He could be saying that believers who are
physically alive will never die in a spiritual sense, but
this too is difficult. Some have said, in connection with
this third idea, that believers who are alive physically
(in contrast with Lazarus who was dead physically) will
never die the "second death" (of Rev. 20:6). Though
all (even pantelists) would agree that this is true, is that
what our Lord is saying here? Although this is a remotely possible interpretation, I offer another one here.
The reason we find this interpretation to be insufficient
is that this is true for those in Christ whether they are
alive *or* dead. There is no reason for Christ to have pointed
out that living believers will not go to hell. Christ is
not merely saying in verse twenty-five that dead believers don't go to hell and then in verse twenty-six that
living believers don't go to hell either. What is the point
in that? If believers don't experience the "second death"
after dying, they certainly would not experience it before dying. Our Lord is teaching something much more
vital than basic perseverance of the saints. He is teaching about the resurrection—which Martha believed in
(11:24)—both in word (vv. 25–26) and in deed (by raising
Lazarus as an example).

If we make the assumption that "he who lives and
believes in me" refers to a believer who has not experienced normal physical death, then we have excluded
the clearest possible referent for "those who are alive."
Look at the connection between the two phrases once
again: "though he die, yet shall he live, and whoever
lives and believes."[29] The nearness of "shall he live" and
"whoever lives" is too powerful to be ignored. They
are speaking of the same thing. This is where Jesus clearly
contrasts the resurrection of Lazarus (which He is about
to perform) with the resurrection of the "last day" that
He had promised so many times before (John 5:29; 6:39,

40, 44, 54). Jesus is saying, "He who gets resurrected on the last day and is a believer shall never experience death," as opposed to those who get resurrected on the last day and are not believers shall experience "death." Why, you may ask, does Jesus specifically refer to the one who "believes in" Him? It is because resurrection is clearly not only for believers. As Jesus already taught (in John 5:24–29), some will be resurrected to "life" (and thus can "never die," 11:26, see also John 8:51), whereas others (who don't believe) will be resurrected to judgment (and thus will "die" in the "second death" of Rev. 20:6). Once again, this is why Jesus points Martha to the necessity of faith in Him (11:25).

### Acts 17

In Paul's speech before the Areopagus, we are told that he mentioned the "resurrection of the dead" to the philosophers, at which point most of them mocked him. At the beginning of this section, we find that the Epicurean and Stoic philosophers heard Paul preaching about "Jesus and the resurrection" and thought he was teaching about "foreign divinities" (17:18).[30] It would be natural to assume that Paul was merely referring to the resurrection of Christ Himself, but the text does not allow us to assume that. Verse thirty-two says, "When they heard of the resurrection of the dead." The Greek word for "dead" is actually in the plural, thus meaning, "the resurrection of all those who are dead." There is nothing in the construction of this sentence that leads us to any other conclusion. Clearly Paul taught them about Christ's resurrection and told them that the "resurrection of all who are dead" was a logical outworking of Christ's resurrection. It is well attested that Greek philosophy did not hold to the physical resurrection of the body,[31] so they naturally would "mock" what Paul said if he meant by "resurrection" what we have been saying all along.

Let us assume for a moment, though, that the pantelist is correct and Paul does not mean a physical resurrection of all men at the end of time. If Paul was referring to the "raising" of the nation of Israel from the deadness of their sins, would he have been mocked? Rather than mocking, they may have been concerned that Paul was preaching there was to be a political revolt of the Jews. The Scriptures show that numerous people were concerned about revolts and uprisings in other instances (John 11:48; Acts 5:35ff; 16:20; 17:6–8; 21:38; 24:5; etc.). There was no reason for the philosophers to mock Paul unless he was preaching the very thing they held as ridiculous and impossible: a physical resurrection at the end of this world.

There are various passages that discuss this topic, so we will not limit ourselves to merely one. Throughout the book of Acts, Paul is heard proclaiming his belief in the resurrection of the dead as merely the hope that existed among the Jewish fathers. If the Jewish fathers can be shown to believe in the pantelist views of a spiritual resurrection, then a major hurdle has been passed by the pantelist (though this does not automatically negate the physical resurrection). If, however, it can be shown that the Jewish fathers, as well as the Jews of Paul's day, held to the physical resurrection as we have presented here, then an insurmountable hurdle has been put in the path of pantelism.

Let us first look at the various passages where Paul uses this line of defense:

> But when Paul perceived that one part were Sadducees and the other Pharisees, he cried out in the council, "Brethren, I am a Pharisee, a son of Pharisees; with respect to the hope and the resurrection of the dead I am on trial." (Acts 23:6)

> But this I admit to you, that according to the Way, which they call a sect, I worship the God of our fathers, believing everything laid down by the law or written in the prophets,

> having a hope in God *which these themselves accept*, that
> there will be a resurrection of both the just and the
> unjust. (Acts 24:14–15; emphasis added)

> And now I stand here on trial for hope in the promise made
> by God to our fathers, to which our twelve tribes hope
> to attain, as they earnestly worship night and day. And
> for this hope I am accused by Jews, O king! Why is it
> thought incredible by any of you that God raises the dead?
> (Acts 26:6–8)

We ask here, what is this "hope" of "resurrection" that
the Pharisees held to, but the Sadducees did not (see
Acts 23:8)? It would certainly be easy for pantelism to
assert that it is a hope of national revival (based on Ezek.
37),[32] but is this what Paul is referring to here?

In 23:8 we find that the Sadducees didn't believe
there was a "resurrection, nor angel, nor spirit," and
therefore Paul appealed to the Pharisees, who did believe in these things. The Sadducees held to only the
first five books of the Bible, which they claimed didn't
teach these three things. Let us ask the pantelist: can
we find a "national" or "spiritual" resurrection (or revival) mentioned in the books of Moses? Yes, among
many others, there is the clear reference to a "national
revival" in Deuteronomy 30:1–10 and a "spiritual revival" in Deuteronomy 30:6.[33] If the resurrection the
Sadducees did not believe in was not found (to their
satisfaction) in the books of Moses, then what was it
that they denied if not the orthodox teaching? In addition, Jesus, in responding to the Sadducees, does not
appeal to any kind of "national" or "spiritual" revival
but those of actual life after death (see Luke 20:37ff).

In Acts 24:15, Paul says the resurrection he believed
in was of the "just and the unjust." If Paul were referring to a "national revival" of Israel, then what do the
unjust have to do with this? A revival of the unjust would
mean that the wicked were to rise up in power as well

as the righteous. If, on the other hand, Paul was speaking of a "spiritual revival," then, once again, how are the wicked resurrected "spiritually?"

Finally, the context of Paul's statement in Acts 26 includes his reference to the physical resurrection of Christ (26:23). If this were essential to Paul's preaching, and thus central to the reason he was in trouble, then the statement in 26:8 that "God raises the dead" (note that "dead" here is plural—it refers to more than just Christ) must be connected to the resurrection of Christ. The burden of proof is upon the pantelist if he wants to say Paul is speaking of two different kinds of resurrection here, especially when we realize that he uses the same terminology in close context with no clear change of topic.

This is sufficient to cast strong doubt on the pantelist denial of a future physical resurrection. There is, however, another facet to this argument that demands our examination. It is well-known that the Pharisees held to a physical resurrection of all men at the end of time. This is attested to in numerous locations by various authors, both ancient and modern, as well as by the Pharisees themselves in their writings.[34] This fact must be taken into account when we consider the defense that Paul gives of his belief in the Final Resurrection. The Rabbis even went to such lengths as to propose there was a bone in the spine that survived the decay of the body and that from this bone the new body grew. In spite of the ridiculous contortions they went through to prove their concept of the resurrection, there is no doubt they believed in a physical resurrection of men.

With this in mind, is it probable or even possible that Paul would have appealed to the Pharisaic hope of a physical resurrection and say that he was on trial for believing the same thing they did (Acts 24:15)? It would be not only foolish (because he would be promoting an errant doctrine) but also a lie (because he would be saving his neck by saying he believed what the Pharisees did when it was not true). Now it is possible the Pharisees also held to a "resurrection" other than the physical one, but if this is so, why does Paul not distinguish which one he agreed with? If Paul did not believe in a future resurrection of all who have died at the end of the world, then he could not take the chance, on so many occasions, of not only being misunderstood but also of promoting false doctrine.

Once again we find that the Scriptures support the traditional teaching of orthodoxy. Knowing the background of the beliefs of the Pharisees (who were the Church's opponents) makes it highly unlikely that Paul (or anyone else for that matter) would have appealed to them for similarity in belief unless it was so. In fact, with the obviousness of the Pharisee belief in a physical resurrection, the authors of the New Testament would have gone out of their way (like the pantelists are doing today) to show that what they believed was not the same as what the Pharisees taught. Simple and unqualified statements like "resurrection of the dead" and "resurrection of both the just and the unjust" were too easy to be misunderstood and used without qualification. Clearly what the entire early Church believed was that there was to be a physical resurrection of all men who ever lived at the end of the world.

### Our Resurrection and Christ's

This final point probably represents the greatest difficulty for the pantelist denial of the orthodox resurrection. Throughout the New Testament, we find that the resurrection Paul personally waited for was intimately related to Christ's resurrection (which we know was a permanent, physical resurrection). In some instances the two are even equated. For the pantelist to minimize our resurrection to something nonphysical is a radical truncating of the doctrine of the resurrection. Let us look at some of the passages that make this association:

> Christ must suffer, and that, by being *the first* to rise from
> the dead. (Acts 26:23; emphasis added)

> We shall certainly be united with Him in a resurrection *like
> His.* (Rom. 6:5; emphasis added)

> He who raised Christ Jesus from the dead will give life to
> your mortal bodies also through His Spirit which dwells in
> you. (Rom. 8:11)

> And God raised the Lord and will also raise us up by his
> power. (1 Cor. 6:14)

> If Christ has not been raised, your faith is futile and you are
> still in your sins. Then those also who have fallen asleep in
> Christ have perished.... For as [all] in Adam die, so also [all]
> in Christ shall be made alive. But each in his own order:
> Christ the first fruits, then at his coming those who belong
> to Christ. (1 Cor. 15:17–18, 22–23)

> Knowing that he who raised the Lord Jesus will raise us
> also with Jesus and bring us with you into his presence.
> (2 Cor. 4:14)

> [Christ] will change our lowly body to be like his glorious
> body, by the power which enables him even to subject all
> things to himself. (Phil. 3:21)

There is no doubt that the authors of the New Testament viewed our resurrection (however we interpret
that) as being vitally connected with Christ's. Even
pantelists acknowledge this fact. The only reason we
are able to have a resurrection is because Christ was
resurrected. The simple question we ask is this: does it
make sense that we have only a nonphysical resurrection because Christ had only a physical one?[35] The one
does not automatically follow the other, and thus it would
be a weak argument for Paul and others to base our

resurrection on Christ's if they were not of the same nature. Yes, Christ's physical resurrection bought us our spiritual regeneration (even though this is not the primary argument of the New Testament), but that is not all.

In the first place, what is the reason for calling Christ the "first" to rise from the dead (Acts 26:23) if there were no others who were going to rise as He did? He must have been the "first" of others who were also going to rise in the same way that He did. This also applies for the reference to Christ as "first fruits" in 1 Corinthians 15:23. He must be the "first fruits" of a "crop" that is of the same extent.[36] As noted before, some pantelists have said that a crop that is harvested thousands of years after the "first fruit" is ridiculous, but in like fashion a crop that is harvested forty years later is just as ridiculous in agricultural terms (even canned goods don't last that long). The point of the comparison is not the length of time but the guarantee of the coming crop being just as complete and good as the "first fruits."

In Romans 8:11, if the "mortal bodies" of believers were given life in A.D. 70, why do we still sin? Is "life" all it means to be delivered from sin? This is another pitiful reduction of the idea of deliverance from sin. The context in 1 Corinthians 6:14 is perfectly clear. Verse thirteen speaks about the physical bodies of believers in Corinth. Verse fifteen also points out the physical bodies of believers (it is not the "body of Christ" as the Church that Paul is concerned about being united to a prostitute). Thus, if verse fourteen (which is practically quoted in 2 Corinthians 4:14) refers to the fact that "God raised the Lord," which meant clearly His physical body, then what would our natural conclusion be about our being "raised" up? The context clearly refers to a physical resurrection for all saints.

Likewise we find the same usage in Philippians 3:21.

In verses ten and eleven of the same chapter, Paul mentions that he wants to know the "power of [Christ's] resurrection" and thus "attain to the resurrection of the dead." The "power" of His resurrection is evident in Paul's life in various ways. Paul shows the "power" of God in living out the "righteousness from God" (3:9), but it is also the same "power" we see connected with our resurrection from the dead elsewhere (1 Cor. 6:14). In fact, Paul says again in 3:21 that it is this "power" that He will use to raise us up. The context is again clear here. "Our lowly body," which will be made like His "glorious body," is obviously our physical body as seen above. Why would Paul equate "our body" with "Christ's body" if he were speaking about the Church as the body of Christ? That would mean Paul said God will make Christ's body to be like Christ's body. In addition, the Church is *Christ's* body; it is not *our* body! To refer to the Church as *our* body is not only incorrect, it is also close to blasphemy; anyone who really thinks the Church is his (or even ours collectively) is probably not a Christian.

### 1 Corinthians 15

Finally in 1 Corinthians 15, we find Paul's most extensive argument for the resurrection of the bodies of individual Christian saints. Much of what needs to be said here has already been said above, so I will not repeat it here. There are some specific things that need to be pointed out though. The first point is the same one we find in the above passages: once again our resurrection is centered and based in Christ's; they are made two parts of a whole—the first assumes the rest will follow (15:23).

In 15:18 Paul says that those who "have fallen asleep in Christ have perished" if the dead are not raised. Why would this be so? If people live on as spirits in heaven after death, why would the lack of a "raising to vindica-

tion" or a "national revival" on earth make them perish? If, however, Paul is referring to their bodies falling asleep (as Jesus did with Lazarus in John 11:11–13),
then without a physical resurrection their bodies would
"perish." Souls cannot "perish" except in hell, so why
would a Christian be concerned about someone in Christ
going to hell?

Later Paul explicitly states that he is speaking about
the resurrection of our physical bodies. In 15:38–39
he says,

> But God gives it a body as he has chosen, and to each kind
> of seed its own body. For not all flesh is alike, but there is
> one kind for men, another for animals, another for birds,
> and another for fish.

Is Paul here speaking about nonphysical bodies? Of course
not. He is speaking about the bodies that all living things
have. His use of "flesh" here clearly cannot be referring to fallen sinfulness, because though animals are fallen
with creation, they do not sin. The question Paul is
answering makes this most evident. He himself proposed
the question, "With what kind of body do they come?"
(15:35). He then goes on to say that the "glory" of our
resurrection body is unlike the "glory" of our present
physical body.[37] He describes our present body as
"physical" and our resurrection as "spiritual" (15:44).
Because he earlier used the image of "seeds" dying and
being sown anew (15:36–37), it is evident Paul is not
saying that presently we have a physical body, but in
the resurrection we will not (our physical body does
not die and grow anew as a spirit, our spirit exists "within"
our physical body. If our physical body dies, it must
grow into another physical form). When Paul calls our
resurrection body "spiritual," he means (as with most
other usages of this term) our resurrection body is related to the Holy Spirit (which makes perfect sense,
see Rom. 8:11). It is a "spiritual" body because the Holy
Spirit of God brings it to life.

Our fallen physical body comes first, and our raised resurrection body comes from that one (15:46). We now bear the image of fallen Adam and will someday bear the image of raised Christ (15:49, see also 1 Jn. 3:2). Does it make sense that we bear the physical (and fallen) image of Adam but will not bear the physical (and resurrected) image of Christ? If we bear the physical fallen image of Adam, we will also bear the physical raised image of Christ.

When Paul then says that "flesh and blood" cannot inherit the kingdom of God, he does not mean that we will be in spirit alone when we are resurrected. The kingdom of God that he refers to is the "eternal kingdom" that Peter also spoke of (2 Pet. 1:11), our existence in eternity after the resurrection. "Flesh and blood" do not refer to the physical nature of our bodies but rather to the weakness of our bodies (see Matt. 16:17; Eph. 6:12; Heb. 2:14), which must be changed before they can reside personally with God for eternity.[38]

It is impossible to find a nonphysical resurrection in this passage. The language does not allow it, the comparisons with Adam and Christ do not allow it, and the rest of the Scriptures do not allow it. We must seek to have a proper understanding of the resurrection, for as John says, "every one who thus hopes in him purifies himself." Hope in the orthodox understanding of the resurrection has a purifying effect on the soul.

### Sleeping Saints

The reference in 1 Thessalonians 4:14 to saints who had "fallen asleep" brings us to our next topic: the New Testament description of dead saints as "asleep." It is clear that the authors of the New Testament used the term "sleep" to refer to death in numerous instances. But does "sleep" refer to the state of the soul or the body? If the pantelist is correct that there is no physical resurrection, then "sleep" must refer to the soul since the body will never "awaken." (In the pantelist scheme of things, the body dies and remains dead forever; the existence of the soul is the only eternal reality, just like in ancient Gnosticism.) This does not hold up under careful scrutiny though. There are two very clear passages in Scripture that describe the state of the soul after death. In Luke 16:19–31, Jesus tells the story of Lazarus and the rich man after they died. We do not need to recount the details of the story. It is sufficient to point out that throughout the story both they and Abraham are conscious and are speaking to each other; they cannot possibly be described as "asleep."

The second text is even more clear. In Revelation 6:9–11, we read of the "souls" of saints in heaven. They are said to "cry out" (6:10) because they had been "killed" (6:11). The point is obvious. They were not asleep. They were very conscious, especially of events on earth.

From this we can see that the term "sleep" can only be referring to the physical body. The soul is not described as asleep after death, the body is. In fact, James specifically says that the "body apart from the spirit is dead" (James 2:26). He does not say the spirit is dead, but the body; the body falls "asleep," not the soul. The body will be awakened (resurrected) on the Last Day, not the soul. It is the soul that waits for the body to be awakened.

This truth heightens the usage of "sleep" that we find in other texts. Jesus is the "first fruits of those who have *fallen asleep*" (1 Cor. 15:20; emphasis added— notice how this verse assumes that Jesus, too, "fell asleep") because He died physically as do all saints, and as He was resurrected physically so will we be. Otherwise "falling asleep" for saints means they have "perished" (15:18), and then the definition for "sleep" must change between Jesus and His saints. If only the soul survives death, then indeed the body (an essential part of the human person since creation) perishes.

## Conclusion

One vital question must be asked here of the pantelist:[39] If the authors of the New Testament *did* want to teach a future physical resurrection, how else would they have said it? If the pantelists are correct in their interpretation of phrases like "raise mortal bodies," "resurrected from the grave," "though they are dead, yet shall they live," "the resurrected cannot die anymore," "raised like Christ," "mortals bodies becoming immortal," and "the dead in Christ shall rise," then no way is left for them to have expressed a truly physical resurrection, even if they wanted to.

The inconsistency of this is clear when we remember there were numerous resurrections in Scripture that were definitely physical (see 1 Kgs. 17:17ff; 2 Kgs. 4:32ff; 13:21; Matt. 27:52ff; Luke 7:12ff; 8:49ff; John 11:43ff; Acts 9:37ff; Acts 20:9ff; Heb. 11:32), and the descriptions of those events used the same terminology we find in the contested passages. To reinterpret each and every one of these references not only goes against the rest of the Scriptures, it also makes the Scriptures into a "code book," where standard words and phrases are used in a such a way that they become cryptic and almost impossible to decipher.

*Notes:*

[1] What we mean specifically by "difficult" is that it is difficult for the pantelist to come up with an event in A.D. 70 that can be said to fulfill the resurrection. It is true that Jesus came in 70 (against the apostate Jews), and it is true that He brought judgment at that time (also against the apostate Jewish nation), but inserting a "resurrection" into that event is truly the most difficult aspect of pantelist thought. There are numerous interpretations of the resurrection by pantelists (many of which contradict each other), which proves that they themselves find it difficult to figure out how to make the resurrection a past event.

[2] See King, Max, *Old Testament Israel and New Testament Salvation* (Warren, OH: Eschatology Publications, 1990) p. 55ff.

[3] Notice how Paul here says that "sin came" into the world and "death [came] through sin, and so death spread to all *because* all men sinned" (emphasis mine). Sin coming into the world brought death. If they were the same thing, then one cannot bring the other. Physical death is a consequence of sin; all men sinned, therefore all men die.

[4] I have not yet found any pantelist who says that "death" always means spiritual death and that we thus don't die physically. Although this has been attempted by "Christian" Scientists, I don't believe the pantelists would go this far.

[5] Even the pantelist *must* distinguish between physical and spiritual resurrection, or he has forced himself to deny the physical resurrection of Christ. In addition, it will not do to say arbitrarily that all references to Christ's resurrection are physical while others are spiritual. Not only is there nothing in the Scriptures to support this claim, we also have to deal with the numerous resurrections done by the prophets, apostles, and by Christ Himself.

[6] The references to sin that do occur in this passage are actually supportive of our position. In verse seventeen, Paul says we are in our sins "if Christ has not been raised" (thus we are *not* in our sins). In verse thirty-four, Paul refers to the sin of denying the resurrection (which the pantelists are guilty of, even though they deny this). Finally, verse fifty-six refers to the "sting of death" as "sin" (thus connecting sin and death in a fashion similar to what the pantelists claim is always the case). The pantelist claims that here is the proof that the resurrection occurred in A.D. 70 when "death" was done away with. If, however, he wishes to maintain this claim, he must also assert that "sin" was done away with, and thus believers no longer sin. In doing so he has grabbed the proverbial tar baby.

[7] The "death" referred to in 4:11–12 is so clearly a metaphor for the sufferings that Paul describes in 4:7–9, as a result of "carrying in the body the death of Jesus" (participating in His sufferings—as

in Rom. 8:17), that we do not even consider this reference anywhere near to what the pantelist refers to as a spiritual resurrection.

⁸ See King, *Israel and Salvation*, p. 64ff.

⁹ Although there is little in the context of this passage to prove that it is referring to the physical resurrection, we believe this is the correct interpretation because of the similarity in wording with other passages that are clearly speaking of a physical resurrection (as Rom. 8:11 and 2 Cor. 4:14).

¹⁰ We do not deny that there is also the description of Ezekiel in chapter thirty-seven where he uses the image of resurrection to denote Judah's release from Babylonian exile. This is, however, not the normal usage of the idea of resurrection. In addition, would Ezekiel use an image (like physical resurrection) to give a promise of restoration to the people if that image were something that they did not believe in or had never heard of before? Although there is a remote possibility of this, it is highly unlikely that when he desired to encourage the people, he would have used an image that was ridiculous to them.

¹¹ Once again we acknowledge the pantelist claim that the resurrection is the restoration of the nation of Israel but reject it as wholly insufficient as an interpretation of numerous texts.

¹² ἀποκτέννω, which is a variant form of ἀποκτείνω.

¹³ ἀπόλλυμι.

¹⁴ *BAG*, p. 95.

¹⁵ As per King, *Israel and Salvation*, p. 52ff.

¹⁶ As per Crews, *Prophecy*, p. 159; emphasis original.

¹⁷ Therefore this text is not specific enough to determine the timing of the resurrection either for the pantelist position nor for the preterist. The only clue we are given is that it *may* be an event that people who are not yet born would experience.

¹⁸ οὐδέ γάρ ἀποθανεῖν ἔτι δύνανται. Note also the use of οὐδέ in the sense of "no longer" or "not any more" in Matthew 5:13, Luke 16:2, and Revelation 12:8.

¹⁹ Notice how, in another context, John says that Jesus was "making himself equal with God" (using the full form ἴσος as opposed to the contract form found in Luke 20:36) in John 5:18. Yet this does not mean that since Jesus had a physical body that God the Father also had to have one. They were only equal in the point of comparison; for Jesus and the Father, equality of Godhood; for resurrected saints and angels, equality of eternal life with God.

²⁰ As per Leonard and Leonard, *The Promise*, p. 178.

²¹ Note the use of γάρ in verse thirty-six, meaning "cause or reason *for*" *BAG*, p. 151; emphasis original.

²² Notice the connection here with what Paul says in 1 Thessalonians 4:16 about Jesus' "cry" and "call" that He gives at the resurrection.

[23] One could compare the present possession of eternal life with possessing a sum of money, while the future participation in eternal life after the Resurrection is more like actually spending the money. Just as we would not say that someone who wasn't spending money didn't actually have it, so also you don't actually have to be experiencing eternal life to "have" it.

[24] See Leonard and Leonard, *Promise*, p. 48ff, where they confidently state that "the present reality of the kingdom of God *seems* to merge with the eschaton" and that it is possible that John's usage of the resurrection "*might suggest* that . . . the parousia [along with the resurrection] is not future history but the church's continuing eucharistic worship" (emphasis mine). No evidence that this is what John intends to teach is given. They merely assert that it appears that way to them; they do not truly deal with the text itself.

[25] See Crews, *Prophecy*, p. 359, where he asserts that those who disagree with him "would make all biblical things literal and physical" with no qualification or clarification. Does this mean he thinks we want to make the Holy Spirit physical? He is a "biblical thing" is He not?

[26] Russell, *Parousia*, p. 126f. One of Russell's major errors is that he assumes that since the word "last" occurs in the Bible in connection with the last days of Israel, every time the word "last" shows up it must be referring to the same thing. Is there nothing else the Scriptures can say regarding its "last time"? According to Russell, the apostles had "technicalized" the word "last" to the point where it cannot refer to anything but A.D. 70.

[27] This is true despite the vague and glib statements of some pantelists that make it appear as though Martha were wrong and Jesus actually *did* correct her by saying there was no future physical resurrection. See Leonard and Leonard, *Promise*, p. 49.

[28] As we will see below, this "living" in verse twenty-six may be assumed from verse twenty-five to be the same thing.

[29] " . . . ζήσεται, καὶ πᾶς ζῶν . . . "

[30] It is most probable that they took "Jesus and the resurrection" (Ιησουν καί τήν ἀνάστασιν) as two separate gods that Paul was referring to, and since they had never heard of them, they wanted to hear "something new" (17:21).

[31] For more on this see Edersheim, Alfred, *The Life and Times of Jesus the Messiah* (Peabody, MA: Hendrickson, 1993), p. 178.

[32] I do not in any way deny that Ezekiel 37 speaks of a spiritual revival of Jews. I do, however, assert that this is not what Paul is speaking of here.

[33] The Sadducees would still not have to believe in spirits to hold to the "spiritual revival" of Israel mentioned in Deuteronomy 30:6. To them it would mean "you will become more lively in serving God."

34 See Edersheim, *Life and Times*, pp. 218–19, 748–49; Lightfoot, John, *A Commentary on the New Testament from the Talmud and Hebraica* (4 Vols., Peabody, MA: Hendrickson, 1997) vol 2, p. 286–288, vol 3 p. 366; Lohse, Eduard, *The New Testament Environment* (Nashville, TN: Abingdon, 1976) p. 59–60, 194–95. Josephus, *Wars of the Jews*, 2.8.14 and the note there, Josephus, *Antiquities of the Jews*, 17.1.2–4.

35 If the "spiritual resurrection" that we receive is really better than the physical one that orthodoxy holds to, then not only were the Gnostics right after all, but Christ only got a "second best" resurrection!

36 Christ's pre-resurrection body was the same as Adam's pre-fall body: able to be tempted. But just as Adam fell and brought us lower than the creation state (sinful), Christ rose and has guaranteed that we will be made higher than the creation state (sinless). If Christ has already given us all the salvation we are to receive, then Satan won at least part of the battle; sin remains in us and will never be totally driven out until after death (which was the same as before the cross—dead saints don't sin).

37 Note here how Paul says that our present body has glory (15:40) just as he also does in Rom 8:30.

38 "'Flesh and blood' are by a usual synecdoche, put for the whole human nature. . . . [T]his expression is used, because it is not human nature as absolutely considered, but as mortal, passible, subject unto infirmities and death itself, that is intended." Owen, John, *An Exposition of the Epistle to the Hebrews* (Carlisle, PA: Banner of Truth Trust, 1854 [1991]) from the works of John Owen, 23 vols. Vol 19, p. 438.

39 This is basically the same question asked of those who reject the preterist understanding of the Scriptures when they say, "If the authors of the New Testament *did* want to say that certain things were near, how could they have made it more clear? How else could they have said it?"

## Appendix A to Chapter 5

# Stevens on Resurrection Bodies

IN A RESPONSE TO A SHORT ARTICLE AGAINST PANTELISM BY Kenneth Gentry, Ed Stevens has stated that Jesus' resurrection body was not a "pure physical body"[1] and that His body had properties that were different from ours in respects other than mere immortality. With this we agree. Where has a preterist ever maintained that Jesus' body was merely a revived version of His body which had died? He further maintains that our resurrection bodies will be both spiritual *and* physical.[2] Again, I do not disagree. In this book and others which are similar, the references to "physical bodies" denote the essential physical aspect of the resurrection body *in contrast* to those (including many pantelists) who would promote an eternal existence in the spirit alone.

The issue, however, is not this alone. Stevens has created a false dichotomy in proposing the only options are a "pure physical body"[3] and a "spiritual and physical body" (which he wrongly says is exclusively the view of pantelism). In essence Stevens is saying that either you are a pantelist or you have the wrong view of resurrection. Stevens says the creeds overreacted to the gnostics by saying the resurrection body was "purely physical."[4] Yet Stevens needs to show where any of the ecumenical creeds say that the resurrection body is "purely physical" and has no spirit to indwell it. Is he really suggesting that the authors of the creeds ignored James 2:26?

Paul's claim that our resurrection bodies are "spiritual" (1 Cor. 15:44) must be compared with his usage of the term "spiritual" in other places (especially those in 1 Corinthians). By doing so we can see that Paul uses the term "spiritual" not to speak of something that is nonphysical (either solely or predominantly) but rather of something that is intimately related to the Holy Spirit—that is, it is "Holy-Spiritual." Stevens further claims that "physical death is the natural consequence of being human" and that therefore our bodies must "see corruption."[5] This is his attempt to avoid the fact that Jesus, in redeeming us from "death," will redeem us from physical death as well as spiritual death. The fact that physical death is the result of the Fall has been mentioned above. Let us merely ask where the Scriptures say that physical death is the result of being human. Death (both physical and spiritual) is not the result of being human but of being fallen humans. Thus if Jesus redeems us completely from the Fall, He will also redeem us from the consequences of the fall.

Later, Stevens asserts that before A.D. 70, the saints had to wait to receive their resurrection bodies, but now they receive them immediately upon their death, because he says (as above) "physical death seems to be a planned, 'natural' consequence of being human and living on earth."[6] He speculates (since he has no biblical foundation for support) that all living saints presently "have" their resurrection bodies but don't "rise with" them until their death.[7] He takes this approach based on Paul's seed analogy in 1 Corinthians 15:35ff, but he never interacts with the rest of the passages about the resurrection and how this fits with them. What do the other passages say? Do any of them describe resurrection as an event that is repeated millions of times? No. Nowhere does the Bible describe the resurrection as something that will continue to happen for eternity every time a saint dies. The only options open for Stevens that fit with the testimony of Scripture are either everyone (including not only us today, but also all unbelievers who are also to be "resurrected to judgment") received their resurrection bodies in the first century, or those who received them in the first century were the only ones who will ever be resurrected. Nothing in Scripture allows for a resurrection after the "final" one (whether that occurs in the first century or the last).

Scripture does not say that on Resurrection Day believers who are alive will receive the "seed" of their resurrection bodies; it says they will "rise" with them. Resurrection will be experienced by all believers. With the number of times that the resurrection is referred to in Scripture, it is amazing there is not one place that we are told that on the day of resurrection the living saints will *not be resurrected* but will instead have to wait until they, too, die in order to receive their resurrection body. Paul, who (according to pantelism) believed confidently that he would live to see the day of resurrection, never once takes the time to point this out. Such a crucial doctrine as this[8] cannot be relegated to a shakey interpretation of an analogy (as Stevens does with 1 Cor. 15:35f) and a vague one-word description like "changed" (1 Cor. 15:51). Would Paul merely say "changed" in order to describe this fantastic process that Stevens refers to? All of this seems painfully implausible.

In fact, death is always portrayed in Scripture as a horrible and unnatural experience; it is never seen as something that God lovingly created as a blessing for the believer. If the pantelist wishes to appeal to Philippians 1:21–24 or 2 Corinthians 5:1–4, he still has serious problems. Paul is not, in either of these passages, referring to the experience of saints after 70, but *before*. This is clearly the same as the experience for us today. Since the day Christ ascended into heaven (not since A.D. 70 alone), believers have been ushered immediately into the presence of Christ at their death. Pointing to texts that appear to place the dead saints apart from Christ before A.D. 70 does not negate the clear texts which place them with Him. If Christ was apart from the saints before 70 (as Stevens asserts) then why would Paul "desire to depart and be with Christ" (Phil. 1:23)?

The final problem with this perspective on the resurrection is that we are constantly told that our resurrection will be of the same quality as Christ's (1 Cor. 15:23, etc.). Yet according to Stevens, our "resurrection" body is not actually resurrected at all. When we die, we immediately receive a "resurrection body" (which is entirely different from our present body), while the body we had in this life remains in the grave forever. By this explanation it would be deceptive for Paul to say that we will be resurrected—our soul does not die, so it cannot be resurrected after physical death; the body that dies stays in the grave and is never resurrected; and the "resurrection body" that we do receive was never dead and so cannot be said to have been resurrected. This doesn't sound like Christ's resurrection at all. One of the biggest proofs that Christ was resurrected was that His tomb was *empty* (John 20:6–7). In other words, the very body that He had walked this earth with had been resurrected and changed into an immortal body. Only the same body would still have the nail prints in it (see John 20:27). The very fact that saints' bodies remain this day in their graves proves that Stevens' errant "resurrection" is entirely different from that of Christ's. The only option for resurrection being an experience for believers immediately at death that accords with Jesus' resurrection is that the very same bodies would be resurrected to immortality (exactly like Jesus' body). Show me the empty graves and I will believe it.

It would not be enough, however, to find the graves of Christians empty, for unless Stevens is postulating a Final Day of Judgment for unbelievers, they too must receive a "resurrection body" at death (John 5:29). Every grave in the world would have to be empty! If, however, Stevens tries to hold onto his concept of an unresurrected "resurrection body," then our only conclusion at this point is that when God "resurrects" the lost, He has created one of these special and wonderful immortal bodies just like our for them to live in (in Hell) for all eternity.

With the wealth of Scripture that points to the resurrection as a single, universal, unrepeatable event like Christ's, we are hard pressed to fit Stevens's idea of resurrection in Scripture.

*Notes:*

[1] Stevens, Edward, *Stevens Response to Gentry* (Bradford, PA: Kingdom Publications, 1997) p. 23f.

[2] Ibid.

[3] Where does "Gentry [say] we are raised physically and then *later* changed into that ultimate spiritual body" (emphasis mine), as is claimed on page twenty-five of the above cited article?

[4] Ibid.

[5] Ibid., p. 26.

[6] Ibid.

[7] Ibid., p. 28.

[8] A doctrine that describes the death-experience of every Christian who lives after A.D. 70 cannot be called anything other than "crucial," especially since it involves the vast majority of Christians, whereas what Stevens says happened in A.D. 70 involves a small minority.

## Appendix B to Chapter 5

# Harden and Noe on Resurrection

IN A HELPFUL, RECENT BOOK,[1] R.C. SPROUL DEFENDS PRETERISM against pantelism (which he refers to as "full preterism"). Shortly thereafter, two pantelists—Daniel Harden and John Noe—produced booklets criticizing Sproul's discussion of the resurrection.[2] Here I'd like to interact with their *main* claims, and since both of these pantelist booklets take basically the same position, I'll deal with them at the same time. I'm glad to say that some of what I said in my preceding chapter on Resurrection does not refer to these two gentlemen. Both Harden and Noe (along with Stevens) have come closer to orthodoxy than most of their pantelist brothers. In regard to this, I am thankful. Unfortunately, as is often said, "close only counts in horseshoes." Close to orthodox is still unorthodox. They are to be considered "close to orthodox" because they acknowledge that the resurrection has something to do with what happens to us and our bodies (contrary to most other pantelists), or else the point of our similarity to Christ's resurrection is moot. This attempt, noble as it is, is still fraught with inconsistency and confusion.

### Resurrection Examples

*Resurrection Order.* To begin with, Harden and Noe claim the "body" we receive in our resurrection is a new body that is given to us by God; it is related to our present body but is not the same one. This, they assert, is what all Christians have been receiving upon death since A.D. 70. Prior to 70, the blessed dead had to wait in Hades apart from God, but at 70 Christ came and took them with Him to heaven. From that point on, all saints, at death, go immediately to be with Christ and receive their new resurrection body. To support this claim of continuing, multiple resurrections, Harden and Noe appeal to the "we" references in Scripture (1 Cor. 15 and 1 Thess. 4), which appear to them to refer to the first century generation only.[3] They argue that Paul's reference to the resurrection of "each in his own order" (1 Cor. 15:23) means that each person who dies after A.D. 70 will be resurrected immediately at death.[4]

The text reads as follows: "But each in his own order: Christ the first fruits, then at his coming those who belong to Christ." But it's easily evident that the only "order" that exists within the passage is twofold, not manifold as Harden and Noe assert. The general word order of the Greek in the passage is as follows: "But each in their own order, [the] firstfruits [is] Christ, then those of Christ in His coming." "Those of Christ" is one collective group that is raised at the same time.[5] The only sense of order Paul is referring to is that our resurrection does not happen at the same time as Christ's; it occurs (collectively for *all* those who are of Christ) at the time of His "coming," not separately for each of us individually. Is there any possibility of slicing up "those of Christ," who are supposed to be raised at the time of "His coming," into literally billions of resurrections over the history of the world? Paul, to be supporting the pantelist claim, would have to have said something like, "But each in his own order, Christ the first fruits, then those at His coming, and all who come later (not at His coming, but) when they die." But there's nothing like this in the text. One has to read pantelist assumptions into the text.

*Daniel's Prophecy.* Along with many pantelists, Harden and Noe also argue that Daniel 12:1–2 predicts that the final resurrection will occur in the first century. Daniel writes:

> At that time shall arise Michael, the great prince who has charge of your people. And there shall be a time of trouble, such as never has been since there was a nation till that time; but at that time your people shall be delivered, everyone whose name shall be found written in the book. And *many* of those who sleep in the dust of the earth shall awake, some to everlasting life, and some to shame and everlasting contempt. (Dan. 12:1–2; emphasis added)

Daniel is later told:

> [G]o your way till the end; and you shall rest, and shall stand in your allotted place at the end of the days. (Dan. 12:13)

First, others have already adequately defended the view that "Michael" is an angelic name for Christ.[6] With this in mind, we are driven to ask: what "arising" of Christ is being referred to in verse one? In verse thirteen, Daniel hears that he too will "stand" (or "rise," NAS), as would "Michael." Interestingly enough, the word used here by Daniel to refer to Christ "rising" or "standing"[7] in 12:1 happens to be the same word he uses to refer to himself "standing" "at the end of the days" (12:13). Closeness and context require that whatever "rising" is done by Christ will likewise happen to Daniel (probably around the same time). If Christ is "rising up" to fight against apostate Israel (in A.D. 70, as most believe), then Daniel is doing the same. If, however, the reference speaks of Christ's resurrection, then Daniel is told he would experience the same thing.

This is not, however, all that is said in the context. The inclusion of "many wakening from their graves" in Daniel 12:2 adds even more to the equation. Interpreters by and large see this verse as referring to the final resurrection. I don't share that view; I also, however, do not agree with the pantelists. Daniel 12:2 says too much to be the final resurrection, but it also says too little to be the pantelist "resurrection" of A.D. 70.

The association between something Christ does in the first century with this resurrection is too clear to miss. There is nothing in the text to support Daniel talking about the first century (12:1) and then without warning jumping to the last century of history (12:2). Pantelists, however, have no interpretive advantage here. Harden and Noe both say that everyone who had died before 70 experienced a pantelist "resurrection" in that same year. The problem with associating Daniel 12:2 with that view is that the verse says too little for that. Look at the difference between the following verses (emphasis added):

> And *many* of those who sleep in the dust of the earth shall awake, some to everlasting life, and others to shame and everlasting contempt. (Dan. 12:2)

> [T]he hour is coming when *all* who are in the tombs will hear his voice and come forth, those who have done good, to the resurrection of life, and those who have done evil, to the resurrection of judgment. (John 5:28–29)

Is there similarity? Yes. But, once again, similarity does not denote identity. We must recognize that Daniel said *"many"* will awake, and Christ said *"all"* will come out of their tombs. Daniel does not use the word "many" to mean "all" anywhere in his book. What event could he possibly be prophesying? In Matthew 27:52–53, we find an event that fulfills exactly what Daniel said:

[T]he tombs also were opened and *many* bodies of the saints who had fallen asleep were raised and coming out of the tombs after his resurrection they went into the holy city and appeared to many. (emphasis added)

Notice how Matthew tells us that "many" bodies were resurrected, not "all" (as in John 5), nor a few. Matthew knew that this event (recorded in no other gospel and thus often ignored) was the fulfillment of Daniel 12:2. These saints were not merely revived as Lazarus was; they awoke to "everlasting life" (Dan. 12:2), never to die again.

Thus the "rising" or "standing" of Christ in Daniel 12:1 refers to His resurrection, and the "awakening" of the saints in Daniel 12:2 refers to the saints whose "bodies were raised out of the tombs."[8] Matthew points out that it was the saints' bodies which were raised (not souls alone), and it was from their "tombs" (not from Hades). Unless we define away what Matthew and Daniel say, we cannot miss how they are both pointing to the resurrecting of bodies to eternal life that had been dead for more than Christ's three days. These saints received their resurrected and glorified bodies long before the rest of us as a special blessing of God (and most probably ascended to heaven by the time that Christ did).

Additionally, note what Daniel is told about himself. In Daniel 12:13, he is told that he will be one of the saints who will be raised in that day. Daniel (whose body was decayed and returned to dust) was raised by Christ, and His body changed so that it was now eternal and could never die, so that he could walk the earth and appear to people in Jerusalem. In fact, Daniel points this very fact out when he says that the raised saints (as well as the wicked) are sleeping "in the *dust* of the earth." This not only points us to the physical, literal graves of dead bodies, but also to the fact that the bodies had returned to dust (both locationally and biologically). Yet Christ's resurrection was so glorious that right after it occurred a number of saints were raised too.

Harden tries to claim that the resurrection of Daniel 12:2 is referring to A.D. 70 alone because "Daniel 12 firmly joins the abomination that causes desolation with the resurrection."[9] What he ignores is that Daniel had easily connected the destruction of the temple (A.D. 70) with Christ's death (A.D. 30) in Daniel 9:25–27. No one believes Christ really died and began the New Covenant in A.D. 70. So why should anyone believe that the resurrection of the *many* saints of Matthew 27:52, prophesied in Daniel 12:2, would have happened in A.D. 70? Daniel readily connects the beginning and end of that forty-year period because they are a part of each other.

So, yes, there was a resurrection of *many* people in the first century, and it was a physical and spiritual resurrection. Pantelists like Harden and Noe often complain that those who hold to the orthodox view of the resurrection make it out to be physical only. Although this may be the case of some who don't understand the orthodox teaching, it is not the case with most. The Scriptures reveal to us that when a spirit is reunited with its original body, it is both a spiritual and physical event because both a spirit and a body are involved. Additionally, it is *spiritual* because the Holy Spirit is involved (Rom. 8:11).[10] In Christ's physical resurrection in the first century, there were *many* saints who were raised also; their spirits were returned to their bodies (as happened to Christ), and their bodies were healed of all their infirmities (as also happened to Christ).

In this vein, Noe asserts that only Christ was promised that His body would not see decay, as per Psalm 16:10.[11] This claim means something for those who are already pantelists but nothing to anyone else. The fact that our bodies are said to "return to dust" is not something that was true before the fall. Noe's citation of Genesis 2:7[12] is greatly misleading. He places it after his quotation of Genesis 3:19 as though it were something God stated *before* Adam had fallen. It was not, however, the state of things before the fall. It was a part of the curse, which came only after the fall (Gen. 3:19). What Genesis 2:7 does say is that man was created from the dust of the ground (something the orthodox do not deny). When he was created, God "breathed into his nostrils the breath of life," and he "became a living being." Although Genesis 2:7 does not say enough to either support or refute pantelism, the assumption of the statement is that the body had the potential of death but not the guarantee.

The similarity between Daniel 12 and John 5 is powerful. The resurrection of the many in A.D. 30 (not 70) was Christ's paradigm of the final resurrection. Just as much as the tomb of Christ was empty, so also were the tombs of these saints. And just as much as they were empty, so will ours be when we "hear his voice" and "come forth" from our "tombs" (John 5:28–29). Noe's claim that the resurrection of the many in Matthew 27 is a "partial but literal fulfillment"[13] of John 5:28–29 is not only unsupportable (making "all" the same as "many"), it is also more confusing than helpful. Few things can be clearer than the fact that Matthew 27 and John 5 are related (both talk about physical resurrection of dead bodies out of their graves), but they are not speaking about the same event.

The pantelist may also try to say this event is talking about A.D. 70, not 30, because of the phrase "end of the days" in Daniel 12:13. As mentioned above, the reference to "the end of the days" does not necessarily refer only to A.D. 70; both Hebrews 9:26 and 1 Peter 1:20 refer to Christ's *first* coming as being at the "end." Additionally, there is nothing wrong with Daniel referring to Christ's resurrection in 30 (12:1a), then to the tribulation in 70 (12:1b), and then to the saints' resurrection in 30 (12:2). He has already done this in chapter nine. There he tells about the crucifixion (9:26a), the destruction of Jerusalem (9:26b), and the New Covenant's institution at Christ's death (9:27). He can jump back and forth because the events are related: Christ's unjust death necessitates that He punish His betrayers.

In fact, when Harden claims Hymenaeus and Philetus could not have taught that the resurrection was past if Paul and others had been teaching a resurrection "based on a changed *physical* body,"[14] his stace is completely unfounded. He goes so far as to say that their error "*couldn't* have arisen"[15] if our understanding of the resurrection is what Paul taught. The most logical reference to Hymenaeus's and Philetus's claims is the *physical* resurrection of *long decayed bodies* of Old Covenant saints that occurred right after Christ's resurrection. Paul did not criticize their understanding of the nature of the resurrection (2 Tim. 2:17–18), because they were correct. (They would have known about the resurrection of the many in Matthew 27.) But they obviously believed that what happened in 30 was all that was to occur. Paul knows we all will receive the same as they received and so points them out to be heretics. Literally, Paul says that they were teaching that the "resurrection already happened." They clearly believed the resurrection of the many was the fulfillment of *all* the resurrection promises. Paul knew there was more to come.

Noe calls what I am saying the "bones-are-still-in-the-graves-objection." Fine. The problem for Noe is that he accepts it for Christ's resurrection, yet he rejects it for ours (and obviously for the many saints of Matthew 27). He claims that if Paul believed what we do, he could easily have run to the local graveyard to refute Hymenaeus and Philetus (2 Tim. 2:17–18), yet he did not do so. True. He also did not go to a tomb to prove Jesus' resurrection. Rather he argued from the Scriptures and commanded "all men everywhere to repent" (Acts 17:30). The reason the "bones" objection works for Christ is because His "flesh and bones" (Luke 24:39)[16] were resurrected; if our resurrection is "like" His, then we, too, naturally expect the same thing.

*Seed Analogy.* Both Harden and Noe refer to the "seed analogy" that is brought up by Stevens.[17] Here they assert that Paul was teaching that our present body is a seed out of which grows our resurrection body. I won't repeat my previous criticisms of this argument. Yet the "seed analogy" doesn't just work for us. It works for Christ as well; that is Paul's point in 1 Corinthians 15. Christ's body (not His soul) that died was only a seed of the (same) body that was resurrected! Since this occurred for Him, it will also occur for all those who are His (1 Cor. 15:22).

It is often hard to tell just what Noe is saying as he tries to explain the "seed analogy." Sometimes it appears as though he is saying our body is the seed;[18] other times it appears as though he is saying our spirit is the seed and our body is only the shell of the seed.[19] The problem with this entire situation is that he is trying to develop a doctrine out of an analogy (which, although he himself acknowledges to be dangerous, he proceeds to do in a highly speculative manner). It is one thing to develop a doctrine out of one passage of Scripture; it is another thing to develop a doctrine out of an analogy. All that can legitimately be gathered from Paul's analogy of the seed in 1 Corinthians 15:35–41 is what Paul himself says:

> So is it with the resurrection of the dead. What is sown is perishable, what is raised is imperishable. It is sown in dishonor, it is raised in glory. It is sown in weakness, it is raised in power. It is sown a physical body, it is raised a spiritual body. If there is a physical body, there is also a spiritual body. (1 Cor. 15:42–44)

Paul here explains the "seed analogy" by saying that our body is "sown" (buried) in a state of being subject to death and then later "raised" in a state of being not subject to death. The translation "physical" (RSV) or "natural" (AV) is greatly misleading. The word Paul uses here also appears in 1 Corinthians 2:14, where it means unregenerate[20] and not corporeal, as opposed to noncorporeal.[21] A literal rendering of the word would actually be "soulish," which is held by various scholars.[22] Now when Paul is comparing "soulish" bodies with "spiritual" bodies, how can we possibly imagine that he is comparing this present mortal body with a different, future immortal body? He is rather referring to the present fallen state of our bodies and the future redeemed state of our (same) bodies. The seed *becomes* the plant, at which point there is no longer a seed. Our bodies will be resurrected (by the power of God), at which point there will no longer be fallen bodies but only redeemed bodies. Our spirits are redeemed by being regenerated; they are not replaced by new spirits. In the same way, our bodies will be redeemed by being regenerated not by being replaced with new bodies.

## Redefining Resurrection

One final point must be dealt with here, and that is the assertion by Harden and Noe that "resurrection" does not refer to what happens to our present bodies, but rather what will happen to our souls at death. In their scheme, "resurrection" means that our souls will be "raised" out of Hades. For the saints who had died before A.D. 70, this happened at the coming of Christ in that same year. For us, this happens when we die.

This redefinition is replete with difficulties. Ironically, they attempt it while simultaneously asserting that their position is the only one that does not require a "metaphorical 'redefinition' of resurrection."[23] Let me begin by pointing out a few of these difficulties, and then I will proceed to show how Scripture clearly rejects this notion of resurrection.

First, since they have defined "resurrection" to mean "going to Hades and coming back out,"[24] they have, by definition, excluded everyone who dies after A.D. 70 from the resurrection.[25] How have they done this? Remember that, by their interpretation, Hades was already thrown into the lake of fire in A.D. 70. If Hades has been done away with and emptied, then either Christians don't go there at all anymore, or they must first go to Hell and then be delivered from it. Obviously they are claiming the first option. But if this is the case, then post-70 Christians don't actually get "resurrected," since "resurrection" means (by pantelist definition) to go to Hades and be freed from it. This makes our experience of entering heaven so entirely different from Christ and the pre-70 saints that we cannot possibly call it "resurrection" but rather "transition," or perhaps "reincarnation." By their own admission, our experience is one of "bypassing Hades" and going directly to heaven.[26] In fact, if resurrection only refers to being delivered out of Hades, then our transition from this life to the next needs a different term entirely.

Second, we should ask what happened to the lost in A.D. 70. Were they freed from Hades and then subsequently returned to Hades when it was cast into Hell? Is this an appropriate description of the "resurrection" they are to experience? John 5:28–29 portrays the lost as being resurrected just as much as the saved. The fact that it distinguishes between a resurrection of "judgment" and of "life" does not mean that the lost do not experience resurrection. In addition, what happens to the lost today? Rather than "going to Hades and coming back out," we would have to say they go to Hades and stay. Is this a raising or a falling?

A third difficulty is found in their understanding of Christ's resurrection from Hades. Harden and Noe state

numerous times that Christ was delivered from Hades
and that this is the fulfillment of His resurrection.[27]
His physical resurrection was merely a means God used
to prove that Christ had actually come out of Hades.
If, however, "resurrection from the dead" means coming out of Hades, then we have a contradiction in terms.
Christ was resurrected *from* the dead *to* life, not from
one place in death (Hades) to another place in death. It
is specifically stated by John that Christ prophesied the
resurrection of His "body" and not His soul from
Hades (John 2:19–22).

Fourth, neither Harden nor Noe would deny that
Christ's actual physical body that died on the cross was
resurrected to life eternal. Yet their common assertion
that the term "resurrection of the body" never occurs
in the Scripture creates problems for them.[28] Noe even
says that since this and similar terms do not occur in
Scripture (which is true), they "do not accurately describe resurrection."[29] Does "Trinity" accurately describe the three-and-one nature of God? It does not
occur anywhere in Scripture. "Resurrection of the body"
is a perfectly appropriate way of describing what the
authors of Scripture are referring to since (1) Jesus'
resurrection, which ours is patterned after, was clearly
a bodily resurrection; (2) the authors of the New Testament use the terms for "resurrection" and "raising"
that were used for Christ's resurrection of His body
to also refer to our resurrection without any qualification or distinction. Being how the term "resurrection"
was so commonly associated with physical resurrection
of the dead, the apostles would have gone out of their
way to distinguish what it was they were talking about
if they did not mean resurrection of bodies.

Fifth, the phrase "resurrection of the dead" (which
occurs in Scripture often) must refer to a resurrection
of something that is dead. The souls of the righteous in
Hades are not lifeless. They are alive. So what is "dead"

that is "raised"? It can be nothing but their bodies, exactly as is so often said in Scripture (Matt. 27:52–53; John 5:28–29 [what else is in "tombs" but bodies? the spirit went elsewhere at death]; Rom. 8:11, 23; 1 Cor. 6:13–15). Yes, it is true that the phrase "resurrection of the body" does not occur in Scripture, but then neither does the phrase "resurrection of the soul," which is what Harden and Noe want to assert is happening.

Finally, they claim that when Christ was resurrected, He took with him some saints out of Hades into heaven. These saints went to heaven with Him but were only allowed to stay on the "outskirts" of heaven and not actually come into the full presence of God. Those who were not taken had to remain in Hades until A.D. 70 when they were resurrected to heaven. Now, however, we go directly to heaven without going to Hades and enter into the presence of God immediately upon death, something the saints who died before 70 were not allowed to do.[30] With this in mind, what was the expectation about death of the New Testament authors during the time between A.D. 30 and 70 and whether there was any difference between what they expected in that time and what the pantelist says can be expected today? First, we find that the apostles expected to be completely with Christ if they died before 70 (not waiting somewhere on the borders of heaven). Second, we find they expected that this experience would be without a body of any form. Third, we find they give no clear distinction between this experience and any future experience of death by later Christians.

Let us begin with Paul's expectation for a starting point:

For to me to live is Christ, and to die is gain. If it is to be life *in the flesh*, that means fruitful labor for me. Yet which I shall choose I cannot tell. I am hard pressed between the two. My desire is to depart and *be with Christ*, for that is far better. (Phil. 1:21–23; emphasis added)

Paul says here (in about A.D. 60) that if he died, he knew he would be "with Christ." He does not say "my desire is to depart and go to Hades." Yet this should be what he would have said if he agreed with Harden and Noe. What else could "be with Christ" possibly mean if it doesn't mean to be in heaven? Even if he expected a special bodiless state (before 70, and thus contrary to pantelist claims) on the "outskirts" of heaven, he could not have said "with Christ," but rather something like "in heaven—but only near to Christ." His reference to "in the flesh" (cf. also Phil. 1:24) clearly says that he believed there was a bodiless existence in heaven *before* A.D. 70 for the righteous.

The apostle John describes the "souls of those who had been slain for the word of God" (Rev. 6:9) as being under the altar. Harden tries to say these saints were in heaven but weren't in the Holy of Holies with Christ because the altar is not in the Holy of Holies.[31] He ignores the fact that they are under the altar, not because they can't go to the Holy of Holies, but rather because they are offering prayers on the heavenly altar (see also Rev. 8:3–4) in the true tabernacle (see Heb. 8:2 and Rev.15:5–8). This group is related to the multitude that John said "are *before the throne of God*, and serve him day and night *within his temple*" (Rev. 7:15). Now if they are "before the throne," then they are in the Holy of Holies, because that is where Christ is seated at the right hand of God. And being there is the same as "serving him day and night within his temple," which is what the saints in 6:9 are doing. Thus John also sees uncountable numbers of saints in heaven, before 70, with Christ.

The author of Hebrews also gives us this portrayal of after-death experience in the A.D. 30 to 70 interim. He says that in his day (before 70), we could "with confidence draw near to the throne of grace" (4:16), something that could not be done before A.D. 30 because Christ had not yet gone into heaven. The souls of all the righteous were taken out of Hades in 30, not in 70. That is what is meant by Christ leading "a host of captives" when He ascended to heaven (Eph. 4:8); to say that this refers to only a few of the righteous in Hades is unfounded and must be inserted into the text.

The author of Hebrews also says that in his day Christians can go into "the inner shrine behind the curtain, where Jesus has gone" (6:19–20), and once again that is pre-A.D. 70 (see also 7:19 and 10:19–22). There was no doubt in his mind that this was the case now that Christ the high priest had entered into heaven on our behalf (in A.D. 30, not 70). Even if the author is only referring to worship on earth in spiritual terms (and we do not believe that it can be limited to this reference), how can we say that unperfected men can spiritually go into the Holy of Holies before perfected (cf. Heb. 12:23) men can go into the true Holy of Holies in heaven? We can only go into the Holy of Holies to worship now because Christ has paved the way for us. We go in both now and after death as a result of what Christ did in A.D. 30, not what He did in 70. Yet when we go in after death, it is only in a bodiless state until the final resurrection of all, which is still in our future.[32]

What have we seen here? Harden and Noe have attempted to redefine both the nature of the resurrection and the bodies that we receive in that resurrection. Their attempt has been as a result of their assumption that the resurrection is not a future event for all mankind. We have also seen that this redefinition (which was necessary in order to maintain pantelist assumptions) was unnecessary. It was unnecessary because the Scriptures do not assume that the resurrection was an event that took place in A.D. 70, and Scripture also describes the final resurrection so specifically that it cannot be anything other than the orthodox explanation of a single, final day in which all men are resurrected to their eternal habitations.

*Notes:*

¹ Sproul, R.C., *The Last Days According to Jesus* (Grand Rapids, MI: Baker Books, 1998).

² Harden, Daniel E., *Overcoming Sproul's Resurrection Obstacles* (Bradford, PA: Kingdom Publications, 1999). Noe, John, *Your Resurrection Body and Life Here, Now, and Forever* (Fishers, IN: The Prophecy Reformation Institute, 1999).

³ For more on the "we" issue, see chapter six under the heading "1 Thessalonians 4." I show there that "we" *does not* always refer to the writer and his readers.

⁴ Harden, p. 77; Noe, p. 49ff.

⁵ The fact that Paul mentions only a twofold order necessitates that *all* that is going to happen in the "resurrection" take place "at his coming" and not at two different times. Pantelists often claim that all those not dead in 70 received a "change" (including, evidently, those not yet born) but do not *actually* receive their resurrection body until they die. Paul does not allow for this in the passage; all who are Christ's are resurrected "at his coming" and not later.

⁶ See Chilton, David, *The Days of Vengeance* (Tyler, TX: Dominion Press, 1987) p. 311ff. Most of the early reformers also held this view (see the notes in the Geneva Bible *in loc.*).

⁷ "arise, appear, come on the scene," in Brown, Francis, *The New Brown-Driver-Briggs-Gesenius Hebrew and English Lexicon* (Peabody, MA: Hendrickson, 1979) p. 764.

⁸ Obviously the wicked dead who were raised to "everlasting shame and contempt" (Dan. 12:2) were not referred to by Matthew because they did not appear to many in Jerusalem, as did the saints. They probably went immediately to punishment, similar to Korah and his followers (Num. 16:30–33).

⁹ Harden, p. 55.

¹⁰ Notice how Romans 8:11 says that the Spirit will give life to our "mortal bodies." He doesn't leave our "mortal" (subject to death) bodies in their graves and give us new bodies; He takes our mortal bodies and gives them life so they cannot ever die again.

¹¹ Noe, p. 71.

¹² Ibid.

¹³ Ibid., p. 34.

¹⁴ Harden, p. 65 (emphasis original).

¹⁵ Ibid. (emphasis original). In reality, pantelism "couldn't have arisen" if the pantelists had taken into consideration the perfect example of the general resurrection that was given to us by God in Matthew 27.

¹⁶ Notice that Christ describes His resurrection body as "flesh and bones." It sounds a lot like a physical body—one that has been redeemed from death.

[17] See previous appendix for more on this.

[18] Noe, p. 67.

[19] Ibid., p. 68f.

[20] Another way of rendering the word here is "without the Spirit" (as per NIV), showing that the essence of the word denotes the fallen, unredeemed state.

[21] The usages in James 3:15 and Jude 19 (the only places in the NT outside of 1 Corinthians) also support this truth.

[22] Richard Gaffin, for one example.

[23] Harden, p. 60.

[24] Ibid., p. 58.

[25] Harden does make reference in this context to the "many" saints of Matthew 27 but says that they were "freed from Hades, but were not yet able to proceed to the Most Holy Place in heaven" (p. 59). He completely ignores the significance of this passage for the definition of "resurrection" and makes the assertion that this group supports his claims, without any biblical support. Here is another example of a pantelist speaking "ex cathedra."

[26] Ibid., p. 59.

[27] Harden, p. 58; Noe, p. 41.

[28] Harden, p. 9; Noe p. 61.

[29] Ibid.

[30] See Harden, p. 58ff; Noe, chapters three, four, and five.

[31] Harden, p. 59.

[32] This point in itself is an answer to the baseless claim that only pantelists can say in their funeral theology that Christians "go to heaven." You don't need to be resurrected to go to heaven.

**Chapter Six**

# The Final Advent

IN THE FIRST CENTURY, THE COMING OF CHRIST TO DESTROY Jerusalem was near at hand. This is why it was such a pertinent topic for the Church. It was going to happen in their lifetime, and thus they saw it as one of the most important topics of discussion. The difference between the first-century coming of Christ and His coming at the end of all things is quite important. In the first century, it was a coming to vindicate Christ and show that He was reigning over all (Matt. 24:30). Christ did bring judgment against the apostate Jews, but it was a vindicating judgment. When, however, Jesus "comes" to bring Final Judgment on all, the primary focus will not be His "coming" but rather resurrection and judgment. He will "come" to the earth to do these things, but the focus of the events in the New Testament is the resurrection and the judgment. The reason we see this distinction is that in the first century, the "vindication" of Christ was a crucial event for the future of the Church. Not only did it prove that apostate Judaism was in error, but it also gave confidence to the Christians and faithful Jews themselves. At the end of this world, there will be no need to "vindicate" Christ; the focus will be His resurrecting and judging all who have ever lived.

With these factors in mind, we should not be surprised to find that there are more references to the

Final Judgment and Resurrection than to the Final Advent. Yet still these passages support the historic Christian view of the end.

## Acts 1

Although Luke makes reference to the ascension at the end of his gospel ("[He] was carried up into heaven," 24:51), the most detailed reference to the ascension occurs in the first chapter of the book of Acts. In this passage, Luke tells us of the questions asked by the apostles, Jesus' response, and the angels' promise of Jesus' return. It is in that promise that we find reference to a coming of Christ that does not fit with the references to His coming against Jerusalem in the first century. The passage reads:

> And when he had said this, as they were looking on, he was lifted up, and a cloud took him out of their sight. And while they were gazing into heaven as he went, behold, two men stood by them in white robes, and said "Men of Galilee, why do you stand looking into heaven? This Jesus, who was taken up from you into heaven, will come in the same way as you saw him go into heaven." (Acts 1:9–11)

Though pantelists attempt various exegetical moves to prove that this passage is speaking of Jesus' coming against the Jews, their attempts are embarrassing. Russell contends that the apostles accepted that they themselves would be the ones to see Him coming "in the same way" without giving any justification for this idea.[1] Crews likewise delves into "nightmare-exegesis." He claims that a physical return of Christ is "too simplistic an interpretation of the verse, and it does not match up with other statements and prophecies in the Bible."[2] We admit that a physical return of Christ does not fit with other prophecies in the Bible: it does not fit with the prophecy of God destroying Egypt (Is. 19:1f), and it does not fit with the prophecy of the future of the tribe of Naphtali (Gen. 49:21). It does not fit with these prophecies because it has nothing to do with them. The only reason one would assume that this prophecy is speaking about the judgment on Jerusalem in A.D. 70 is if he had assumed what the text meant before he read it. There is nothing in this text that points specifically to the punishment of Israel, to Jerusalem, or to the time of the event; all these things must be read into the text.

Crews goes on to try to say that nonpantelists believe Christ was a "physical only" being who became a "spiritual only" being at the time of the ascension. I do not personally know of anyone who teaches this, and I challenge Crews and others to point out any major orthodox theologian who holds to this.[3] After creating this straw man, Crews disassembles it by claiming that Christ only appeared in physical form to the apostles in order to fulfill prophecy (which prophecy, he does not tell). In other words, when He ascended He was in actuality going back to a "spiritual only" state. He no longer has the physical body that was resurrected.[4]

He then alleges that since the ascension was a "spiritual only" event, the thing discussed in Acts 1:11 must be Christ's spiritual return in 70. The weakness of this claim is self-evident. What, though, is the reason that Crews goes through such theological contortions to prove this point? He obviously knows that the Greek words rendered "in the same way" in Acts 1:11 cannot be avoided.[5] The Greek word used here shows a virtually indistinguishable similarity between the two objects. Knowing this, Crews worked hard to assert that the ascension was a "spiritual only" event. He realizes that if Christ's ascension was a spiritual *and* a physical event, then the angels meant that He would return *both* spiritually and physically at some undetermined day in the future. As has been noted by others, Luke is careful to point out how the apostles physically saw Christ's

physical body ascending. He says they were "looking
on," and He was taken "out of their sight" while they
were "gazing into heaven as he went." The angels said
"why are you looking into heaven?" and told them Jesus
would come "in the same way as [they] saw him go"
(Acts 1:9–11).[6] Luke uses as many terms as he can without
overdoing his point. He wants to make it clear that the
apostles saw the physical body of Christ ascend. Now
if Crews is right then Christ must have "shed" His body
sometime after the ascension—where did it go?

Admittedly the main point of the passage (Acts 1:6–
11) is not to prove the physical return of Christ. It is
rather to tell about the events associated with the ascension of Christ. Wanting to give more than a one verse
(Luke 24:51) description of the event, Luke begins by
elaborating on the ascension. In spite of this, Luke's
point cannot be missed that the disciples saw Jesus'
physical body actually "taken up" into heaven (Acts
1:11). This was essential for the testimony that they
were to give to the world. The apostles referred to Jesus'
command that they were to be His witnesses (Acts 1:8)
on many instances (see Acts 2:32; 3:15; 10:39; 13:31).

In one instance, however, Peter claims to be a witness to something that we might find remarkable. In
Acts 5:31–32, Peter says that he and the other apostles
were witnesses to the event where "God exalted [Christ]
at his right hand as Prince and Savior." Now Peter was
not in the throne room of God when Christ was "presented before" God the Father to receive all dominion
(Dan. 7:13–14), therefore what event was he referring
to? He was saying that he saw the ascension of Christ
into heaven, which was the "coming" of the Son of Man
to the "Ancient of Days." Peter was witness to the fulfillment of Daniel 7:13–14, and Luke describes that event
as something that was physically seen. The allusion to
the Daniel 7 passage is clearly seen in the fact that Jesus
did not merely float up into the sky. He was taken up

by a cloud (Acts 1:9), exactly as Daniel said ("with the clouds"—Dan. 7:13).

When in A.D. 70, the apostate Jews "saw" Jesus coming on a cloud (Matt. 24:30; Rev. 1:7), they did not see the ascension of Christ into heaven, neither did they see the exaltation of Christ at the right hand of God. Those events took place forty days after the resurrection in the sight of the apostles alone. What they saw was positive proof that Christ had *already* been enthroned forty years before. Christ's spiritual "cloud-coming judgment" on the Jews in A.D. 70 was proof that He had already come in clouds to be seated at the right hand of God in A.D. 30.[7] If one did not submit to the testimony of the apostles that Jesus had ascended in clouds to the Father in 30, one would have to submit to Christ's "cloud-coming" in 70.

In conclusion we can note that the testimony of both Luke and the apostles was uniform. They acknowledged that Jesus ascended to heaven with His physical body. The promise that He would return in the same way meant that some day Jesus would be seen returning on a cloud. This is why Paul refers to the Final Advent by saying Jesus will come with the clouds in 1 Thessalonians 4:17. This expectation, though not as germane to the context of the first century as the destruction of Jerusalem, was just as firm in the apostles' minds as their belief that Jesus had ascended to heaven before their very eyes.

## 1 Corinthians 15

We have already covered most of this passage in previous chapters,[8] but I need to point out here the specific reference that Paul makes to Christ's coming. In chapter two I focused on an argument from the nature of Christ's reign. Here I focus on His future coming. Paul has already pointed out in 1 Corinthians that there is a coming of Jesus where all Christians will be reunited to Him (and thus he is not speaking of Jesus' coming in

70). Here Paul tells us about a coming of Jesus that will not occur until He has "put all his enemies under his feet" (1 Cor. 15:25). The passage reads as follows:

> Christ the first fruits, then at his coming those who belong to Christ. Then comes the end, when he delivers the kingdom to God the Father after destroying every rule and every authority and power. For he must reign until he has put all his enemies under his feet. (1 Cor. 15:23–25)

In this passage (which contains no references to either Jewish apostasy [unless they are considered as one of Jesus' "enemies"], the destruction of Jerusalem, or a "soon" time frame for the fulfillment), Paul says that the "end" will come (15:24) at the same time that Jesus "comes" and resurrects all the saints (15:23). If we were to assume with the pantelist that every time the Scriptures refer to the "end" or Jesus' "coming" that they are speaking about A.D. 70, we would be guilty of inserting our own preconceived notions into the Scriptures. The "end" is not always the end of Judaism in 70 A.D. Did Peter watch Jesus' trial so that he could see the end of Judaism (Matt. 26:58)? Did Jesus only love the apostles until Jerusalem was destroyed (John 13:1)? Did Paul only want the Corinthians to understand his teaching until A.D. 70 (2 Cor. 1:13)? We would answer "No" to each of these because the context shows that they are not speaking about the end of the Old Covenant in A.D. 70. We must do the same in 1 Corinthians 15:24.

As we are forced in the context of Matthew 24 to acknowledge that the "end" Jesus is speaking of is the end of the Jewish nation, we are forced in this passage to acknowledge that Paul is not speaking of the end of the Jewish nation. In context, what "end" is Paul referring to? As mentioned above, there is no mention of Judaism, Jerusalem, or nearness of fulfillment. In the very next verse, Paul clearly refers to something that will end at a certain point in time: the reign of Christ. He says that the reign of Christ will only continue until "he has put all his enemies under his feet" (15:25). If "*all* his enemies" are not yet under His feet, then simple logic forces us to conclude that Jesus is still reigning. Remember Paul himself said in Ephesians 1:21 that Jesus would still be reigning in our age; therefore, in this age His enemies are not yet all under His feet (1 Cor. 15:24–25). Thus we can only conclude that the "coming" that Paul says must happen at the "end" (the end of His reign) has not yet occurred.

This conclusion has full accord with the rest of the Scriptures, and it avoids the exegetical gymnastics the pantelists go through to assert that the "end" has come because Jesus has finished His reign (while at the same time they acknowledge that He is still reigning). Just as the Lord's Supper continues today because Jesus' physical presence is not with us and will end when He returns physically, likewise we can see that if Jesus is still putting His enemies under His feet then He has not yet "come," as Paul says in 1 Corinthians 15:23. To conclude otherwise forces us into numerous discrepancies that cannot be solved. We would have to assert both that the physical resurrection occurred in the first century (see chapter five for more on this) and that Christ finished His glorious Messianic reign of "this age and the age to come" in forty years (thus putting enemies under His feet that didn't even exist yet!). Once again, pantelism makes the Scriptures not only foolish and contradictory but also virtually impossible to understand.

### 1 Thessalonians 4
One of the difficulties with interpreting this passage is that Paul here uses terms that are similar to those used at times to refer to the coming of Christ against Jerusalem. Difficult, however, does not mean impossible. To

determine the meaning of the passage we must discern certain factors: time references, the contextual topic, and background information. The passage itself reads as follows:

> But we would not have you ignorant, brethren, concerning those who are asleep, that you may not grieve as others do who have no hope. For since we believe that Jesus died and rose again, even so, through Jesus, God will bring with him those who have fallen asleep. For this we declare to you by the word of the Lord, that we who are alive, who are left until the coming of the Lord, shall not precede those who have fallen asleep. For the Lord himself will descend from heaven with a cry of command, with the archangel's call and with the sound of the trumpet of God. And the dead in Christ will rise first; then we who are alive, who are left, shall be caught up together with them in the clouds to meet the Lord in the air; and so we shall always be with the Lord. Therefore comfort one another with these words. (1 Thess. 4:13–18)

Note first that there are no true time references. We say no "true" time references because some wish to say that Paul's reference to "we who are alive" (in vs. 15) means that Paul expected to be alive when Christ came. If one were to ignore the testimony of the rest of Scripture, that conclusion would be possible. Through a careful examination of this idea, along with the rest of Paul's statements about his expectations, we will show that such a reading would be incorrect.

In 1 Thessalonians 4:15, Paul uses the phrase "we who are alive, who are left" to refer to those who have not yet died at the "coming" of Christ. The context of the passage is Paul's response to the Thessalonians regarding the fate of the believers who had died before the "coming" of Christ. He thus is contrasting those "who are asleep" (4:13) with "we who are alive" (4:15).

First, the assertion that when Paul says "we who are alive," he means that he believed he himself would be alive is doubtful. That would mean that Paul was wrong.

He did not live until A.D. 70. He died at the hand of Nero approximately four years before. It would also not do to say that Paul believed he *might* be alive: he says "we who are alive" not "we who might possibly be alive." In other words, this verse says too much for the pantelist. According to their interpretation, Paul believed (and was thus wrong) that he himself would live to see the coming of Christ against Jerusalem.

More contextually, just as firmly as Paul says "we who are alive," he says later, "[Jesus] died for us so that whether we wake or sleep we might live with him" (1 Thess. 5:10). He thus here acknowledges that he may be dead ("asleep") when Christ comes. In fact he goes further than that. He doesn't merely say that he himself could possibly be dead when Christ returns (as though the verse read: "whether *I* wake or sleep"). He says "whether *we* wake or sleep" meaning that it was just as possible that he and all his readers would be dead as it was that they would be alive. If it were possible that all of Paul's readers would be dead at the time of the "coming" of Christ to resurrect His saints, then Paul must have viewed that as an event that could be quite far into the future.

Additionally, Paul states in many places just as emphatically that he and his readers "will be raised" (the same type of phrase used to refer to those who had died in 1 Thessalonians 4:16) as though he is assuming that they will all be dead when Jesus comes to resurrect His saints (e.g., 1 Cor. 6:14; 2 Cor. 4:14). This leads us to conclude that Paul did not know when the day would come that Jesus would return and bring resurrection. He used phrases that could fit with it happening both in his lifetime or long after he died. With this in mind, we must avoid the idea that Paul's "we who are alive" meant that he believed he would live to see the Final Advent; he was just as firm in his belief that he would die first.

It would also be wrong for us to conclude that every time Paul said "we" he meant only he and his readers. There are many instances in the writings of Paul where it is impossible to limit Paul's "we" in that fashion. There are actually four different ways that Paul uses the word "we" in his letters. He can use "we" to refer to himself alone (Rom. 1:5; 3:9 [notice here that Paul does not include others in authorship in 1:1], 1 Thess. 2:18; 3:1 [with 3:5]); he uses "we" in a few instances in which he does *not* include himself (Rom. 3:5 "inflict wrath on us?", 1 Cor. 10:22 [Paul himself was not doing what he told them to stop doing]); he can use "we" to refer to himself and others while excluding the readers (Rom. 3:8; 1 Cor. 1:23; 11:16; Gal. 4:3; 1 Thess. 2:13; 3:12; 2 Thess. 2:13; etc.); and he can use "we" in reference to all true believers (including us today) who ever did or will live (Rom. 4:24; 5:8; 6:4; 15:1; 2 Cor. 5:21; Gal. 2:16; 4:28; Eph. 2:3; Phil. 3:3; 1 Thess. 5:8; Titus 3:3, 5; etc.). Considering that this last usage (all believers of all time) is the most common for Paul, and considering that the context of 1 Thessalonians 4:13–18 clearly portrays a physical resurrection which has not yet occurred, we would be hard-pressed to say that Paul believed firmly that he and his readers are the "we" who would be alive when Christ came.

I am not denying here that 1 Thessalonians 5:1–9 speaks of the readiness that Paul wanted his readers to have in preparation for the Neronic persecution. We are, however, stating that Paul does make a clear switch in topic when he says, "but as to the times and seasons" (i.e., the times and seasons that he and his readers were then in as opposed to the Final Advent which they would not even see). In verse ten, Paul brings together the two topics (of the Final Advent and Christ's spiritual coming against Jerusalem) by saying that "whether we wake or sleep we might live with him." His point of

our "living with him" is an obvious reference back to
the "raising" of believers that happens in 4:16–17; the
fact that Christ "rose again" to life and that we are to
"rise" means that we will "live with him" (see also John
14:19). The reason that they might "sleep" is because
they may not survive the Neronic persecution he was
warning them about. The fact that he has returned to
the topic of resurrection, as found in 4:16–17, is evident by his call to encourage one another in 5:11 that
he repeats from 4:18. His pattern of thought in 4:13–
5:11 is obvious:

> *4:13–18.* Those who have died won't be left out of the
> resurrection, in fact, they will experience it before those
> who remain alive do.
>
> *5:1–9.* You already know that we are soon to endure a
> persecution in which many Christians will be martyred.
>
> *5:10–11.* Thus, whether you are alive or dead, you will not
> miss the resurrection; whenever it happens, even if it is far
> enough away that we are all dead, all Christians will be
> included in it.

Therefore since we find no reference to Israel or
nearness in the context, we are lead to consider the
primary topic to be Christ's physical resurrection and
its consequences for the believer. Paul says in
1 Thessalonians 4:14, "Since . . . Jesus died and rose
again . . . God will bring with him those who have fallen
asleep." We should here be asking, what is this "bringing with him" that God would do? Paul obviously equates
it with the "dead in Christ" (i.e., those "who have fallen
asleep," vs. 14), who "will rise" (i.e., be brought "with
him," vs. 14), that he refers to in 4:16. It is clear that
Paul is using the common euphemism for death when
he refers to believers who have "fallen asleep" (see John
11:11–13). Furthermore, in verse sixteen Paul makes

it clear that he is speaking about physical death. It is there in verse sixteen that Paul uses the exact same word for "rise" that he did when he said that Christ "rose again" in verse fourteen.[9]

Admittedly, the word for "rise" is often used for such things as "standing up" or one's being "lifted up" in position, but the context here is discussing not only the physical death of believers (and the possibility that their death would keep them from participating in Christ's coming) but also the physical death *and* resurrection of Christ (which cannot be reduced to a merely spiritual event). Paul's connection here between the physical dying and being raised that Christ experienced with the same for believers is too close to miss. This is not an event that took place in the first century. Just as we did not claim that Christ was born in the sixth century B.C. because we did not actually see it happen, likewise we do not claim that this "coming" of Christ took place in A.D. 70 because the events that Paul connects with it (e.g., the physical resurrection of all believers) did not happen. To deny this on the basis of the "near" passages is entirely unjustified since there are numerous "near" statements in and around the prophecies of Christ's birth, yet they do not force us to claim He was born in the sixth century B.C.

I do not deny that Paul many times referred to a "coming" of Christ that was clearly referring to His destruction of Jerusalem. That is not in question here. The question is whether the "coming" referred to in 1 Thessalonians 4 is the same one or not. We would be in error if we automatically assumed that every time one of the standard terms was used to refer to the "coming" of Christ, the author was speaking about Jesus' coming in A.D. 70. Paul himself refers to the incarnation (the first coming) of Christ as both a "coming" (1 Tim. 1:15) and an "appearing" (2 Tim. 1:10).[10] The background of the text would have much to do with the

Old Testament that Paul had used to teach the Thessalonians about Christ (see Acts 17:2–3). As seen in the previous chapter, there was clearly an expectation in the Old Testament of physical resurrection that went beyond what happened to Christ (notice also that Luke says one of the main things that Paul told the Thessalonians was that Christ was to "suffer and to rise from the dead"—Acts 17:3).

## 1 John 3

In chapter three of the first epistle of John, we find a reference to an "appearing" of Jesus that will have dramatic consequences. As has been said before, however, the chapter divisions in Scripture are sometimes less than helpful. This is one of those situations. We will therefore pick up our quotation from the last verses of chapter two:

> And now, little children, abide in him, so that when he appears we may have confidence and not shrink from him in shame at his coming.... See what love the Father has given us, that we should be called children of God; and so we are. ... Beloved, we are God's children now; it does not yet appear what we shall be, but we know that when he appears we shall be like him, for we shall see him as he is. And every one who thus hopes in him purifies himself as he is pure. (1 Jn. 2:28–3:3)

As has already been pointed out in chapter four, John is clearly connecting his concept of the "coming" and "appearing" of Christ with "the day of judgment" that he refers to in 4:17. Here, however, we need to examine what it is that John is referring to by the terms "appearing" and "coming," which he uses in 2:28 and 3:2.

Certain basic facts can be deduced from these verses to limit the context of what John is discussing. We can see in 2:28 that there was a concern in John's mind that if his readers did not "abide in" Christ they would be "ashamed" when Christ came. In 3:1 he speaks of how wonderful it is to be "called children of God" and then says that when he was writing it was already true that they were children of God (3:2a, "now"). Though it was already true that they were children of God, it was also true that there was something else which they were to become that they did not yet have knowledge of (3:2b). The only thing known for sure was that since they were to see Christ "as he is" they were to "be like him" (3:2c). Finally, the hope they had of being "as he is" was something that had a purifying effect on the individual believer (3:3).

If we assume the pantelist view of this passage, we find there is a terrific difficulty encountered here. Most often pantelists will merely rush over these passages with a quick statement that they confirm what they have said before.[11] When the passage is clearly examined, we find that it not only does not fit with the pantelist scheme of things, but it also clearly affirms that John believed in a coming of Christ that has not yet occurred today.

One pantelist attempts to prove the past nature of this passage by equating it with a passage that contains similar wording.[12] In 4:17, John gives his readers confidence for the "day of judgment" by saying that "as he is so are we." The pantelist argument goes that since the Christians in the first century were already like him (from 4:16 we see that we are "as he is" in "love"), we too are "as he is." Therefore the statement in 3:2 about being like Christ is a past fulfillment. This argument holds no water. In 4:17, John says we "are" (present tense) like God, and he knows how we are like Him (in love). In 3:2, John says we "shall be like him" (future tense) and that he *does not* know how we shall be like Him. To equate these two ideas is to say that John (and thus God as the author of Scripture) could contradict himself and that when he says something hasn't happened yet, it could have already happened. The nightmare that results from this idea is pure insanity. No word in Scripture would have any meaning at all if opposites can mean the same thing. It is patently clear that John was referring to two different things here; in 4:17 he was speaking of how we are already like God (in love, i.e., spiritually), and in 3:2 he was speaking of how we are not yet like God.

With this passage we see that the pantelist's need to find ways to fit things into the A.D. 70 event once again does not work. Again, I acknowledge that most of the passages in the New Testament that are prophetic refer to the coming of Christ against the apostate Jews in the first century (specifically the passages that have "near" time references).[13] We do not, however, agree that a "near" time reference can be inserted into every prophetic passage in the New Testament, and 1 John 2:28–3:2 is one of those.

1 John 2:28 tells us little about what John believes about the "coming" of Christ that he is referring to. There is no time reference anywhere in the verse; there is no mention of apostate Judaism, nor of a Judaic context of any kind. John's primary (if not sole) focus is the standing of believers when Christ "comes." Hypothetically, verse twenty-eight *could* refer to the shame believers would have (if they had been unfaithful) when Christ was vindicated in A.D. 70 against the Jews, but it more easily refers to every believer standing before Christ (whether in or out of the body) after he dies. The connection, however, of this verse with 4:17 (and the manner in which 4:17 makes it clear that all believers await a personal judgment by Christ Himself) presses us toward seeing this in the light of what Paul has spoken of in 1 Thessalonians 4:13–18: the coming of Christ to resurrect all men. In addition, the closeness of this verse to 3:2 forces us to consider that John is speaking about the same topic (especially when there is no clear

break in topic [as is found in 1 Thess. 4:18–5:1]).

In 1 John 3:1, John is speaking about what is already present for the believers of his day. They were already "children of God." In 3:2 he mentions that there is something that they are yet to be that they do not yet know how to define. John's words are clear that he himself cannot fully describe what this "new" state is to be like. He says we are to be "like him." Being "like him" is obviously something that John and his readers did not already possess. It is future, and John is unable to fully define what it is like. This calls us to look in Scripture for a similar description of "being like Christ" that was not yet a reality for the Christians of the first century. The writings of Paul provide ample evidence for this idea:

> For those whom he foreknew he also predestined to be conformed to the image of his Son. (Rom. 8:29)

> Just as we have borne the image of the man of dust, we shall also bear the image of the man of heaven. (1 Cor. 15:49)

> [T]he Lord Jesus Christ … will change our lowly body to be like his glorious body. (Phil. 3:20–21)

As has been seen above, these verses are all found in the context of the physical resurrection, which has not yet occurred. The connection between these verses and what John is saying is too clear to be missed. Both Paul and John believed that something was to occur in the future that would "conform" us to Christ's image, where we would be "changed" "to be like" Christ. These verses are clearly talking about the physical resurrection that is to take place at the Final Advent.

John was saying in 3:2 that he was unable to describe exactly what our resurrection body would be like. He only knew that it was going to be like Christ's body. Now John had personally seen Christ's body in the days between the resurrection and the ascension, yet he was still unable to describe exactly what that body was like. This is clearly because of the many unusual characteristics that Jesus' body took on after the resurrection: He was not automatically recognized (John 20:15) and was obviously physically different in appearance (John 21:12); He was able to eat (Luke 24:42–43); He could seemingly pass through walls (John 20:19); He still had (and has) the nail scars in His body (John 20:27); and He was unable to die again (Acts 2:24). If we were to see someone like this today (even with all of our scientific "knowledge"), we also would be unable to describe just what kind of a body it was.

In addition, we must recognize that John had never seen anyone other than Christ who was resurrected (who was unable to die again like Lazarus did). Thus he only knows that we will be "like" Christ. We cannot, however, be exactly like Him. He is the Divine Creator, and we are mere human creatures. We can only be perfect humans; God's perfection is certainly beyond the level of perfection that can be found in finite creatures. Although this is not the chapter on resurrection, it was necessary to cover this information first.

What, therefore, does John mean when he says that "we shall see him as he is" (1 Jn. 3:2)? John here uses a particular Greek word for "we shall see" that he has used at other times in this letter.[14] The same word also appears over thirty times in the gospel of John. The predominant usage by John refers to physical sight.[15] In the first epistle of John, there is not a single reference that refers to anything other than physical sight (1:1–3 is especially powerful in this idea).[16] The weight of the evidence for John's usage of this word is that he means that we shall physically "see him as he is" "when he appears" physically, before the eyes of all men. We must remember here that only a select few actually saw the *risen* Christ (Acts 10:40–41). Equally important is the fact that John himself only saw a "vision" of Christ in Revelation 1:12–16, it was not truly Christ "as he is" (unless one supposes that He just did a really good job of speaking with a sword in His mouth [Rev. 1:16]).

One last point must be made here. The word that John uses for "appear" in 3:2 is also used elsewhere in 1 John (see 1:2; 2:19, 28; 3:5, 8; 4:9).[17] In every instance John uses the word for a physical appearance with no note of a spiritual event. In 1:2 he uses the word twice to prove that he physically saw the risen Christ. In 2:19 he refers to the visible recognition of who the falsely professing Christians were in the congregation. In 2:28 he refers to the coming of Christ. In 3:5 and 8, John speaks about the first coming of Christ as an "appearance" (clearly not a spiritual event). Finally in 4:9 he says that God's love (which cannot be seen with the eyes) was "made manifest" by His sending Christ into the world. John is clearly using the word for "appear" to refer to things seen with the eyes, not to something merely recognized in the mind. For the pantelist to say that this refers to the coming of Christ in A.D. 70 because it was also referred to as an "appearing" is inadequate. Similar wording does not imply that the author is speaking about the same thing. In addition, if we say that John believed Jesus' Final Advent to be a spiritual event that does not need to be seen with the eyes, then we must say the same thing about His first coming (and thus go against what John himself says in 1 John 1:1–3). Yes, the first coming of Christ did not need to be seen by all in order to be true (John 20:29), yet the testimony of it had to be given first by those who did see it (see Luke 24:48; John 21:24; Acts 1:8; 2:32; 3:15; 5:32; 10:39, 41; 22:15; 26:16; 1 Pet. 5:1; 1 Jn. 1:1–3).

John once again unites the three essential factors of the Final Advent together in a way that does not fit with the pantelist scheme of things. He believed that

Jesus was going to physically appear before all
(1 Jn. 3:2). At that time He would physically resurrect
everyone (3:2) and bring judgment on all men (4:17).
The burden of proof is once again on the pantelist to
show how this passage either has a "near" time reference or that it refers to a spiritual event rather than a
literal/physical one. There is nothing in this passage that
necessitates that John was here speaking of the destruction
of Jerusalem in the first century, and only a predispo-
sition to see that in the passage would lead someone to
believe that he was. The preponderance of the evidence
is that John believed not only that Jesus would come to
judge Israel spiritually (in A.D. 70), but also that He
would come to judge all men physically at the end of all
things.

Pantelists can and have interpreted these passages
differently, so I do not assume that all pantelists agree
with the "pantelist" positions described above. The point
should be perfectly clear though that however pantelists
interpret certain passages, the standard agreement between them is that there is not to be any future physical coming of Christ to end this present world. It is
that very point that is inconsistent with the Scriptures.
Agreeably, the Scriptures speak more about the incarnation of Christ and His coming against Jerusalem in
A.D. 70 than they do about His Final Advent, yet that
does not make it false. We must remember here that
pantelists need to show that everything in this book is
false in order to defend themselves. By pantelist assumptions, if there is merely one passage of Scripture that
speaks of a future event (even something other than
the Final Advent), then that disproves the basic pantelist assumption. That is very shaky ground to be standing on. This is something orthodoxy does not need to
worry about.

## How Long Do We Wait?

A question that is often asked by pantelists is, "Why do the authors of the New Testament tell their readers to wait for events that won't take place for at least two thousand years?" Their contention is that if the apostles told them to wait for something, then it must be assumed that the apostles knew that what they were waiting for would happen while they were still alive; the apostles would not tell their readers to wait for something that would not happen in their lifetime, would they? An event does not, however, need to be near for an individual to wait for it. In fact it can be something that does not occur for thousands of years. There are many words used in various contexts to refer to waiting, and we find that though they often refer to a short wait, this is not always the case.

But we can ask here, how long did Adam and Eve wait for the coming of the Messiah? Genesis 3:15 states that He was to come from the seed of the woman (easily, and obviously, misunderstood to mean during their lifetime). Yet we know that they waited for thousands of years for Christ, the majority of that time being after they died. There are other verses in Scripture that make this even clearer.

A similar usage of "waiting" occurs in the book of Hebrews. The same word used in James 5:7 to refer to a farmer waiting for crops is used by the author of Hebrews in 11:10.[18] He says that Abraham was waiting for the New Jerusalem, which came in the first century (see Heb. 12:22). Most translations render Abraham's "waiting" as "he looked forward to" because they recognize the extreme length of time involved. Abraham waited for the New Jerusalem, but he did not see it until many years after his death.

This ties in directly with what was said about Abraham earlier in the letter to the Hebrews. In chapter six we are told that Abraham, "having patiently endured, ob-

tained the promise" (6:15). What promise is it that
Abraham waited for and received? In the previous verses
we read, "God made a promise to Abraham . . . saying
'Surely I will bless you and multiply you'" (Heb.
6:13–14). We must ask here though, did Abraham receive this promise during his lifetime? No. Abraham
saw his son Isaac born, as well as other descendants,
but he did not see his descendants as numerous "as the
stars of heaven and as the innumerable grains of sand
by the seashore" (Heb. 11:12). He saw that day long
after he died. Yet the author does not qualify this as a
unique situation of waiting; Abraham waited and received
what he waited for.

When the author says that Abraham (along with
numerous other Old Testament saints) "did not receive
what was promised" (11:39) and that he only saw the
fulfillment "from afar," "not having received what was
promised" (11:13), he is careful to qualify what he says.
He points out that when Abraham "died in faith" (11:13),
he at that time had not received the promise. Pertaining to the physical fulfillment of this promise in the
nation of Israel, Abraham "waited" four hundred years
after his death before he saw that fulfilled; pertaining
to the spiritual fulfillment of this promise, he "waited"
two thousand years after his death. Most clearly though,
since the author refers to Abraham's desire for a "heavenly" city (11:16) as an essential part of the promise, it
is the spiritual descendants in the New Jerusalem that
Abraham waited for more than anything else (again, for
two thousand years!).

Likewise, Jesus says that Abraham "rejoiced that he
was to see" His coming (John 8:56). Yet Abraham had
to wait a very long time before he saw it. Does that
mean he did not wait? No, if anything it means that
waiting cannot be limited either to a short duration or
even to one's lifetime.

This concept of waiting is made even more difficult

for the pantelist when we consider that in chapter ten
the author of Hebrews used the same word to refer to
the fact that Jesus sat down at the right hand of God in
order to "wait until his enemies should be made a stool
for his feet" (Heb. 10:13). The pantelist would insist
that this waiting was a short time (between A.D. 30 and
70), however, the usage of "wait" in 11:10 doesn't allow this assumption. If Abraham can wait for two thousand years to see Christ and the New Jerusalem, then
Christ can wait equally as long or longer (at least Christ's
wait is during His "lifetime"). Abraham waited during
his life and after he died as well; we cannot insist that
waiting cease at one's death. Adam waited thousands of
years to see Christ restore what he himself had lost.

Yes, Paul spoke of the resurrection as something
that he was waiting for, but was he expecting to wait
only a short time? The text of 1 Thessalonians 4:13–
5:10 allows for a great duration of time (5:10—"whether
we wake or sleep"), which could certainly include thousands of years, as it did for Abraham (Heb. 11:10). We
must ask the question here, did those Christians whom
Paul says had "fallen asleep" (4:14) stop waiting when
they died? Did they all of a sudden come into a state
where they had not yet received what they were waiting for in life, yet they were no longer waiting for it?
This is utter nonsense and cannot be supported from
the Scriptures. Waiting can last beyond a person's lifetime and possibly even thousands of years beyond.

*Notes:*

[1] Russell, *Parousia*, p. 147–48.

[2] Crews, *Prophecy*, p. 28.

[3] Ibid., p. 29. Crews gives no support or reference for his opinion that this is the position of any theologian; it is completely unfounded.

[4] We don't have the time or space to delve into a discussion of Gnosticism here. We will, however, note that if the pantelists are right (spiritual is more important than physical, and only the spiritual is eternal), then basically the Gnostics were right. Though I have never seen a pantelist assert this, it would not surprise me.

[5] τρόπος, "Manner, way, kind . . . in the same manner in which=(just) as" *BAG* p. 827.

[6] See especially Gentry, Kenneth, *He Shall Have Dominion* (Tyler, TX: Institute for Christian Economics, 1992 [1997]), p 276.

[7] It must be noted here that Daniel 7:13–14 is not a prophecy of the destruction of Jerusalem (Daniel refers to that in 9:26), it is a prophecy of the ascension of Christ into heaven. Thus Matthew 24:30 and Revelation 1:7 are using the same imagery of Daniel 7 (coming on clouds=divine judgments being made), but they are not referring to the same event.

[8] See chapter three for a discussion of the present reign of Christ and chapter five for a discussion of the resurrection.

[9] ἀνίστημι, which often refers to the physical resurrections that were done in the New Testament: Mark 9:9; John 11:23; Acts 9:40–41, etc.

[10] In 1 Timothy 1:15 Paul says Christ "ἦλθεν," and in 2 Timothy 1:10 he describes the incarnation as an "ἐπιφανείας."

[11] See Crews, *Prophecy*, p. 94 and 141f.

[12] See Crews, *Prophecy*, p. 142.

[13] Pantelists are constantly telling others to "deal with" the time frame references in the New Testament. If this were all that they were saying, they would be preterists rather than pantelists. Unfortunately they are "dealing with" the time frame references themselves in an improper fashion; they take the references to "soon-fulfillment" as a hermeneutical key for all other passages (even those which give a long term time reference). We as preterists have truly "dealt with" *all* passages that have "soon-fulfillment" time references; it is the pantelist who needs to "deal with" the passages that have *no* "near" references!

[14] ὁράω, though here it appears in the future form as ὀψόμεθα.

[15] Only John 1:51; 3:36; 14:7, 9; and 15:24 have any possible connection with a "nonphysical" sight, and even those use "nonphysical" sight in connection with "physical" sight.

[16] Even the reference in 3:6 is probably referring to false apostles who said that they too had seen Christ face to face and that this was

proof of their apostleship. This probably is the reason for John's preface to the letter (1 Jn. 1:1–3); he was giving a testimony of his own apostleship. The letter of 1 John is, after all, a statement of what proved those "who went out from" them (2:19) to have been false teachers.

[17] The word is φανερόω.

[18] ἐκδέχομαι.

# Chapter 7

# Creedal Authority

THE CHRISTIAN CHURCH HAS SEEN NO END TO THE heresies that have arisen. In fact, it is because of heresies that sound doctrine has been more firmly and accurately stated. God is the One who sends the heretics against the Church to test those who are truly faithful and to cast out the unfaithful (Deut. 13). At the times when the Church has been most powerfully attacked by heretics, the Holy Spirit has led her to respond by stating the truth in written format—the creed. This written statement is not intended to supersede the Scriptures but rather to be an authoritative interpretation of them. If a Mormon, a Jehovah's Witness, and a Protestant can all agree that "Jesus is God," then we need a more precise definition of what we mean by that. The Mormon's definition of that statement is "Jesus is (one of many) God(s)." The Jehovah's Witness' definition is "Jesus is (god, but not) God." These definitions do not in any way agree with the historic Christian understanding of "Jesus is God," and thus we need to define more clearly what we mean by the terms we use, which is done with written confessions of faith.

## Private "Creeds"
Everyone who calls himself a Christian has a confession of faith or creed (from the Latin "credo," meaning

"I believe"); no one can consider himself a Christian
and not have one. The situation that is unique today is
that the majority of "creeds" are unwritten. People keep
their creeds in their heads, with the result that (and
sometimes the intent that) they can never be formally
criticized.

Keeping one's creed privately in the mind makes it
very difficult to use. This is why we find evangelical-
ism dying (if not already dead) today. People have little,
if any, organized thought about theology. They merely
throw into their mental creed whatever comes their way,
without ever considering whether it contradicts what
else they believe. No formal criticism (even on their
own) is ever done. In addition, a mental creed causes
people to be unsure of what they believe; it is very difficult to look up chapter and verse in your head unless
you have a photographic memory. I can remember in
seminary when other students would firmly assert two
completely contradictory teachings in the same sentence.
My mind still reels to think that these men are pastors
today.

When pastors have mental creeds and thus teach this
to their people, we find Christians by and large becoming anti-creedal (even if they don't know it). By "anti-
creedal" I don't mean they actively tell people not to
believe anything, but they are telling people not to have
*written* creeds.

In fact, many people who actually have a written
creed (i.e., they belong to a church that claims a creed
as its official statement of faith) live as though all they
have is a mental creed. These are the people who don't
know what their church holds to as official doctrine.
They know merely what they themselves hold to (sometimes) and so far haven't heard anything from the pul-
pit they didn't like. Scores of Christians go on like this
throughout their entire lives. They go to one church
until they hear something they don't like, and then they

leave and start over again. This is not due solely to the fault of the people; it is also (if not more so) the fault of the pastors.

When we assert today the divinity of Christ, we do so by standing on the shoulders of the saints who have come before us. If they had not done the work, if they had merely maintained a mental creed and never clearly asserted their beliefs in writing, each and every Christian would have to sit down and decide for himself what he believed on every issue available. Can you imagine the chaos? If this were the state of affairs for the Church for the last two thousand years, we would still be like infants with no progress in our understanding of the Scriptures (Eph. 4:14).

## Public Creeds and the Final Advent

In the creeds we are confronting an authoritative body, which has, through the illumination of the Spirit, declared the truth of certain doctrines. One individual's private judgment on a particular issue is easy to deny; the unanimous opinion of a group of faithful Christians is much more difficult to deny. If there is anything that can be seen as a unanimous opinion of the Church for the last two thousand years, it is that there will be a personal Final Advent of Jesus Christ, wherein He will bring judgment and resurrection upon all men who ever lived and at that time end the present system of things.

It has been said that "to some degree we all operate under the influence of believers who have gone before us."[1] Though there are numerous "branches" of the Church of Jesus Christ, there is also one broad heritage that all "branches" have, and that heritage is the history of the Holy Spirit working through His people. Richard Pratt has noted that this history has been powerfully seen in the "ecumenical councils of the early church," specifically the Apostles' Creed, the Nicene Creed, and the Council of Chalcedon.[2] These creeds

have defined the parameters of Christian orthodoxy. If
the pantelist wishes to question the accuracy of these
councils as a whole (because they assert the physical
return of Christ at the end of this world), then he must
acknowledge that he is surrendering any grounds for
an "orthodox" faith. He may claim that he still has the
Scriptures as a grounds for an "orthodox" faith, yet by
doing this he shows his similarity to the cults: they too
claim that they interpret the Scriptures correctly, in
spite of their extreme divergence from the historic
Christian faith. If he denies the validity of all creeds,
he must assert that "orthodoxy" is an open ground—
thus allowing any heretic to be considered a true Christian, because there are no limits to his orthodoxy.

If the pantelists wish to call the Church to account
on false teaching, they have picked an area that has some
of the most solid attestation throughout the history of
the Church. They cannot merely assert that the creeds
are not correct and therefore define their "heterodoxy"
out of existence. A common response to creedal assertions is that the Church fathers misinterpreted certain
preterist texts and therefore erred in every point of
eschatology. This argument does not hold water; the
Church fathers also held to baptismal regeneration—
that does not mean that everything they said in regard
to the sacraments is faulty. Making an error in one area
of doctrine does not *automatically* make everything within
that doctrine faulty.

Some have tried to say that preterism is just as much
against the creeds as pantelism is. We must assert that
this is not true. The history of the Church has shown
that new creeds were written to expand upon the previous creeds. What we consider the "ecumenical creeds"
did not reject previous teaching but rather added to it
and expanded upon it. *Expanding* upon a creed in response to a new situation in theological thought is completely in accord with the nature of the creeds and how

they have been written in the past (which is what preterism does). *Rejecting* a major doctrine of the creeds is completely out of accord with the nature of the creeds and how they have been written in the past (and this is what pantelism wants to do). Preterism accepts all that the creeds affirm in regard to the Final Advent and wishes to further acknowledge the spiritual comings of Christ in history. Pantelism denies what the creeds affirm in regard to the Final Advent and wishes to change what the Church has believed for her entire history. These are by no means the same thing.

The reason that dispensationalism is not considered heterodox is because it does not deny any of the essentials as found in the historic protestant creeds. Its adherents are, however, to be considered aberrant because they have added numerous errant teachings to the doctrine of the Final Advent. Some of these teachings (like those found in the Scofield Reference Bible) are derogatory to the orthodox faith (such as the teaching that sacrifices performed in the [supposed] future temple of Israel will be pleasing to God). Although they teach such lies (which in themselves are heresies), they are not heretics because they elsewhere hold to the truth of the sufficiency of the cross of Christ. (They are aberrant because their teachings are contradictory to the orthodoxy they hold to in other areas.)[3]

The Holy Spirit could have allowed the Church to go through her existence without the New Testament (the first Christians had nothing but the Old Testament), yet He chose to inspire the apostles to give us the fullness of revelation in written form. In doing this, He endorsed the written format of doctrinal statement as the one He saw as best for the Church. With this in mind, we can ask one question: how did the Holy Spirit lead the Church in the understanding of the Scriptures? Are there any pantelist creeds? No, the Spirit has led the Church consistently for the last two thousand years to affirm that God has set a day in which Christ will come physically to this earth to resurrect and judge all men.

## Sola Scriptura

It is the Scriptures that we give absolute authority to because they are the very words of God. When the Church examines those Scriptures, she explains what the Spirit leads her to see by declaring those truths in creeds—"when He, the Spirit of truth, has come, He will guide you into all truth; for He will not speak on His own authority, but whatever He hears He will speak" (John 1:13). The creeds are never considered (by the orthodox) to be above the authority of the Scriptures. But they are genuinely authoritative interpretations of the Scriptures. They are certainly not to be viewed the same as any other writing by a Christian, no matter how wise he may be. The creeds are the statement of the faithful Church as a whole, the body of Christ that possesses the guiding influence of the Holy Spirit. This does not assert that the Church, in council, is infallible; I want to make it clear that "all synods or councils, since the Apostles' times, whether general or particular, may err; and many have erred. Therefore they are not to be made the rule of faith, or practice; but to be used as a help in both" (*Westminster Confession of Faith*, 31.3).

Those who have this basic understanding of the position of creeds and the councils that write them could never agree with the pantelists who say, "People who belong to churches which worship using traditional liturgies . . . are not free to question the doctrinal statements found in these creeds."[4] If a congregation holds that the creeds cannot in any way be questioned, then they are in danger of leaving historic Christianity as a whole, let alone Protestantism.

Freedom to question and freedom to begin teaching new doctrine based on novel theological assumptions are, however, not the same thing. We as Christians must work together in a community. There are no "lone ranger" Christians. If we allow either a modern interpretation or an ancient one (as those found in the creeds) to *dominate* our view of the Scriptures, we have a truncated view of truth. Both the past and the present are necessary to help us interpret the Scriptures. Preterism seeks to do this very thing. As preterists, we are seeking to re-examine the past (private) interpretations of certain Scripture passages while we carefully acknowledge that our forefathers may have been trying to teach something they knew was right but which sometimes used the wrong Scripture for the right doctrine (sometimes they did properly understand preterist passages). This can only be done by standing on our forefather's shoulders. As can be seen from the previous chapters, sufficient ground does not exist that would allow us to reject what the creeds say about eschatology, and acknowledging the need to reinterpret certain passages that are undeniably preterist does not lead one to reject everything they said.

The pantelist not only wants to reject the shoulders[5] (thus forcing himself to start at the bottom again), but he also wants to allow his modern interpretation to be a new authoritative mental creed. Thomas and Alexander Campbell sought to rid the Church of "sectarianism" by forming a society of Christians without a creed. Their spiritual children (the Church of Christ) are perhaps one of the most sectarian groups in the world. This is also where some of the largest groups of pantelists are coming from. Pantelists themselves are almost tyrannical in their mental creeds. They are in essence claiming that their unwritten creeds are completely authoritative for interpreting the Scriptures.

There is a crucial point that must be made at this time. Classical Protestantism holds that the "sola" in "sola Scriptura" means that Scripture alone is the *sole infallible standard* of truth. That Scripture is the only *infallible rule* does not, however, mean that it is the only source of truth. To say that Scripture is the only place that truth can be found is to deny Scripture: the heavens themselves reveal the glory of God (Ps. 19:1). If the physical creation itself reveals eternal truth (Rom. 1:20), how much more should we expect to be able to find truth in the authoritative creedal statements of the Church, especially given the fact that the Church is designed by God to be the "pillar and bulwark of the truth" (1 Tim. 3:15) and has been protected from mass theological error by the work of the apostles (Eph. 4:13).

If the pantelist is correct in his interpretation of the Scriptures, then he is also incorrect. If all has been fulfilled by A.D. 70, then Paul's prediction of the soon-coming maturity of the Church, which would protect her against giving in to "every wind of doctrine" (Eph. 4:14) must have been wrong; thus the Church gave in to an enormous wind of doctrine (in the teaching of the Final Advent being future), and therefore we aren't safe from errors of this magnitude even today (maybe the creeds were wrong that God exists?).

## Court and Constitution

None of what has been said above in any way asserts that the councils or creeds are infallible. Yet there must be an authoritative system of checks and balances, or else private chaos would reign. In the Christian community, we are to balance three things and balance them well. We must balance the authoritative heritage of the past, of the present community we live in, and of our private judgment.[6] If we allow any one of these to be dominant over the other two, we will make mistakes (sometimes grave ones) in our interpretation of the Scriptures. The pantelist does not want to get rid of heritage per se, he merely wants to create a new heritage with himself as the head. Because the Protestant Reformation rejected the teaching that tradition and Scripture are equal in authority, this does not mean that it rejected tradition wholesale (that was the error of the radical Anabaptists). The reformation put tradition in its place as the authoritative interpretation of Scripture— "It belongeth to synods and councils, ministerially, to determine controversies of faith" (*Westminster Confession of Faith*, 31.2).

The reformers taught firmly that one of the greatest problems with Romanism was that it ignored the principle of *sola Scriptura*. Yet these same reformers were constantly quoting Augustine, Chrysostom, other fathers, and the creeds. We cannot forget that God created the Church as the "pillar and bulwark of the truth" (1 Tim. 3:15). To assert that the Church has not dealt properly with eschatology for the last two thousand years and has en masse allowed the traditions of men to define doctrine in this area is to assert that the pillar has fallen and the bulwark has been broken down. God designed the Church the way He did in order to protect against errors; did He fail in His design? Two thousand years of unanimous error would say that He did. If we in our sin can be strong enough to thwart God in His plans to protect the Church from radical apostasy, we have little confidence that the Church is right about anything, and we must spend eternity trying to get things right. If, however, God designed the Church correctly, then creeds are a proper part of confessing her faith.

What, therefore, is the relationship between Scripture and tradition? The analogy of a court and a constitution is appropriate here. A court without a constitution could not do much, unless of course it were to start cold with every decision (something akin to rejecting heritage on every issue). Likewise, a constitution without a court would merely sit there and never affect anything. Similarly, if every individual were a court, we would have constant conflict. In our analogy, the one authoritative court is the Church (both past and present), and the constitution is the Bible, an infallible constititution.

With Scriptures being infallible, we have no need or right to criticize them. Although the statements of the court (both past and present) are authoritative and cannot be overturned by private individuals, they can be criticized and corrected by the Court itself. The statements (as we find them embodied in the historic creeds) are the court interpreting an infallible constitution. As the court comments, we accept the authority that the court has, recognizing that the court's authority is subject to the infallible authority of the constitution. If the court of the past is found to be wrong by the court of the present on a decision they made, the present court can go back and criticize them by the constitution (but only when the court itself is in humble submission to the wisdom God gave it and not in a proud arrogance that denies this). The frame of mind that says anyone may, at any time, question the wisdom of our forefathers in the faith merely because he sees fit to, is a radically "American" idea.[7] This modernistic frame of mind which puts forward the wisdom of the individual (or even a particular community) at the cost of all other individuals (or communities) is typical Enlightenment thinking found most clearly in the rugged individualism of America. It is not found in the scriptural understanding of the universal Church of Jesus Christ.

The creeds can be changed but not by rejecting them and writing new ones. That is the path taken by those who are outside of the historic Protestant Church (cults, etc.). The Holy Spirit has brought more unity in the history of the Church concerning the fact of the Final Advent than He has about virtually any other subject. If the pantelists wish to change the Church's position regarding the Final Advent, it will not be done by standing outside the stream of Christian orthodoxy and yelling at those inside. Neither will it be done with the weak arguments and contradictory exegesis of Scripture that they have put forward. The pantelist is standing outside of where he should, with a divisive attitude, throwing broken arrows at the Church; he has little hope of bringing about the change he desires. If people are as undiscerning about pantelism as they have been about dispensationalism, then there may be a similar effect on the Church, but since Christ is putting all His enemies under His feet, pantelism will eventually be put there as well.

*Notes:*

[1] Pratt, Richard, *He Gave Us Stories* (Brentwood, TN: Wolgemuth & Hyatt, 1990) p. 70.

[2] Ibid.

[3] What Scofield gives with one hand,"the fulfillment of the O.T. types . . . through the sacrifice of Christ" (note under Rom. 3:24), he takes away with the other, "these offerings [the ones done in the future in a "rebuilt" temple] will be memorial, looking back to the cross" (note under Ezek. 43:19).

[4] Leonard and Leonard, *The Promise*, p. 75.

[5] Notice though that the pantelist goes out of his way to assert that he is a faithful evangelical; a definition that could not exist without the assumption of the work done by millions of faithful (creed-writing) Christians before us! He chastises us when we say "orthodox," but he wishes to be considered "evangelical"—he wants to tell us not to eat cake while he is stuffing it in his mouth. The pantelist rejects the shoulders when they are inconvenient and do not fit with his predetermined theological grid; otherwise he uses them readily.

[6] See Pratt, *Stories*, chapter 3.

[7] Oddly enough, both dispensationalism and pantelism are predominantly American phenomena. Is this really surprising?

# Scripture Index